ONE WEEK LOAN

This edition first published 2011

© 2011 Parliamentary History Yearbook Trust

Blackwell Publishing was acquired by John Wiley & Sons in February 2007. Blackwell's publishing programme has been merged with Wiley's global Scientific, Technical, and Medical business to form Wiley-Blackwell.

Registered Office

John Wiley & Sons Ltd, The Atrium, Southern Gate, Chichester, West Sussex, PO19 8SQ, UK

Editorial Offices

350 Main Street, Malden, MA 02148-5020, USA

9600 Garsington Road, Oxford, OX4 2DQ, UK

The Atrium, Southern Gate, Chichester, West Sussex, PO19 8SQ, UK

For details of our global editorial offices, for customer services, and for information about how to apply for permission to reuse the copyright material in this book please see our website at http://www.wiley.com/wiley-blackwell.

Library of Congress Cataloging-in-Publication Data

A century of constitutional reform / edited by Philip Norton.

    p. cm

  Includes bibliographical references and index.

  ISBN 978-1-4443-3894-2 (pbk.)

  1. Constitutional history–Great Britain. 2. Law reform–Great Britain–History–20th century. I. Norton, Philip. II. Parliamentary History Yearbook Trust.

  KD3966.C46 2011

  342.4103–dc22

ISBN 978-1-4443-389-4 (PBK)

A catalogue record for this book is available from the British Library.

This book is published in the following electronic formats: Wiley Online Library 978-1-4443-389-4

Set in 10/12 Pt Bembo by Toppan Best-set Premedia Limited

Printed in Singapore by Hó Printing Pte Ltd

1 2011

CONTENTS

LIST OF CONTRIBUTORS

Chris Ballinger was awarded a doctorate at Queen's College, Oxford, for a thesis which analysed government-sponsored attempts to reform the house of lords from 1911 to 2000. He was lecturer in politics at Brasenose College, Oxford from 2001 to 2006; and in 2004, he was successively committee specialist to the house of lords' select committee on the Constitutional Reform Bill [HL] and a visiting research fellow at the Australian Senate. His published work encompasses British and European elections, prime ministers, and constitutional reform, and he has been BBC Oxford's election analyst since 2001. He is currently senior research facilitator in the social sciences division at Oxford University.

Robert Blackburn is professor of constitutional law, and director of the Institute for Contemporary History, at King's College London. Among his many published books on parliamentary affairs are *The Electoral System in Britain* (1995), *The Meeting of Parliament* (Aldershot, 1990), *Constitutional Reform* (ed. with Raymond Plant, 1999) and *King and Country* (2006). He is a frequent contributor of articles on parliamentary subjects for academic journals, most recently on 'The Prerogative Power of Dissolution of Parliament: Law, Practice, and Reform' and 'The 2010 General Election Outcome and Formation of the Conservative-Liberal Democrat Coalition Government', for *Public Law*. He has regularly been invited to give expert evidence to inquiries on parliamentary matters, such as on the government's voting and parliamentary reform proposals during the 2010–11 session for the Lords' constitution committee and the Commons' political and constitutional reform committee. Professor Blackburn is the author of two leading works on the theory and practice of parliament, *Griffith & Ryle on Parliament: Functions, Practice and Procedures* (2nd edn with A. Kennon, 2003), and the volume 'Parliament' in *Halsbury's Laws of England* (5th edn, 2010). He is a member and former academic secretary of the Study of Parliament Group, and a fellow of the Royal Historical Society.

David Feldman is the Rouse Ball professor of English law in the University of Cambridge, a fellow of Downing College, Cambridge, and the president of the Society of Legal Scholars for 2010–11. He was educated at Exeter College, Oxford, and previously taught at the universities of Bristol and Birmingham and the Australian National University. From 2000 to 2004 he was the first legal adviser to the parliamentary joint select committee on human rights, and from 2002 to 2010 a judge (and vice-president, 2006–9) of the constitutional court of Bosnia and Herzegovina. He has been appointed queen's counsel *honoris causa*, elected a fellow of the British Academy and a member of the European group of public law, and held visiting positions at the universities of Melbourne (Miegunyah distinguished visiting fellow, 2006) and Nottingham (Sir J.C. Smith senior visiting scholar, 2010). His writing is mainly in the fields of constitutional law, comparative public law, civil liberties and human rights, administrative law, criminal procedure, and remedies.

Alexandra Kelso is lecturer in politics at the University of Southampton. She is author of *Parliamentary Reform at Westminster* (Manchester, 2009) and principal investigator on an ESRC-funded research project from 2010 to 2012 examining the house of commons' departmental select committee system.

Philip Norton is professor of government and director of the Centre for Legislative Studies, at the University of Hull. His publications include 28 books, including *The Constitution in Flux* (Oxford, 1982), *The Commons in Perspective* (Oxford 1981), *Parliament in British Politics* (Basingstoke, 2005), *The British Polity* (5th edn, Harlow, 2010) and (with Bill Jones and others) *Politics UK* (7th edn, Harlow, 2010), as well as the three-volume series, *Parliaments in Western Europe* (1998–2002). He is editor of *The Journal of Legislative Studies* and has served as president of the Politics Association, vice-president of the Political Studies Association, and co-chair of the research committee of legislative specialists of the International Political Science Association. He was elevated to the peerage, as Lord Norton of Louth, in 1998 and served as the first chairman of the house of lords' select committee on the constitution. He also chaired the Conservative Party's commission to strengthen parliament, which reported in 2000. Apart from serving on various committees in the house of lords, he is regularly invited to give evidence to committees in both Houses as well as committees in other legislatures.

Barry K. Winetrobe is a parliamentary and constitutional consultant. A member of the Hansard Society and the UK study of parliament group, he worked for many years as a senior researcher in the research services of the house of commons and the Scottish parliament. He has taught public law, politics and related subjects at a number of universities, most recently as reader in law at Napier University, Edinburgh, and has been a witness before several parliamentary committees in London, Edinburgh and Cardiff.

Introduction: A Century of Change

PHILIP NORTON

With the United Kingdom lacking a codified constitution, there has been no extraordinary formal mechanism for amending the provisions of the constitution. Change has been achieved through parliament. The century since the passage of the Parliament Act 1911 has witnessed significant constitutional change. The measures enacted have affected basic relationships at the heart of the nation's constitutional arrangements: those between the two chambers of parliament, between parliament and the people, between the state and the individual, between the UK and the rest of the world, and between the centre and the rest of the UK. The measures enacted prior to 1997 were essentially individual statutes produced in response to particular challenges. The period since 1997 has seen proactive and extensive legislation, changing substantially the contours of the constitution. Despite the scale of the change, the measures have been disparate and discrete and not generated within a coherent philosophical framework. Although achieving their principal goals, not all have had the effects intended. This volume treats some of the key measures enacted in this period.

Keywords: constitution; European Union; house of commons; house of lords; human rights; legislation; parliament; referendums

Constitutions, as John Stuart Mill observed: 'are the work of men . . . Men did not wake up on a summer morning and find them sprung up.'[1] Though constitutions do not emerge from the ether, most – since the writing of the constitution of the United States in 1787 – are consciously crafted as specific and codified documents, establishing the institutions of the state and the relationship between those institutions and between those institutions and the people.[2]

The British constitution is distinctive, though not unique, for lacking such codification and is unique in having no particular moment when it came into being. It has evolved over centuries.[3] That evolution has sometimes been traumatic and its development has been uncertain. There is little to sustain a whig interpretation of history. The constitution has changed, at times dramatically, because of the desires of, and conflicts between, particular individuals; the path of constitutional history could conceivably have been very different had Charles I and his son James II been more willing to compromise or if Charles I's military commanders had been more effective. Despite upheavals, including an attempt to craft a republic and a form of written constitution, 'England's political development displayed a remarkable continuity from its medieval roots'[4] and has been

[1] J.S. Mill, *Representative Government* (1968), 177 (first published 1861).
[2] Philip Norton, *The Constitution in Flux* (Oxford, 1982), 3.
[3] On critical junctures in that evolution, see Elizabeth Wicks, *The Evolution of a Constitution* (Oxford, 2006).
[4] Kenneth Dyson, *The State Tradition in Western Europe* (Oxford, 1980), 38.

adapted to meet the demands of a changing, and growing, kingdom. The United Kingdom has emerged with a distinctive form of parliamentary government, albeit one premised essentially on English dominance and norms.[5]

The very nature of the constitution that has emerged, both in terms of its longevity and its form, has created the conditions for its amenability to change. It lacks codification and concomitantly any extraordinary mechanism for amendment. There is no clear or formal dividing line between what constitutes a core component of the constitution and what does not. The constitution has endured in large part because of a supportive political culture and in part because of what Michael Foley has termed 'constitutional abeyances', a tacit condoning of constitutional ambiguity as a means of resolving conflict.[6] Some degree of ambiguity allows a constitution to adapt to the demands of the time and to the evolving wisdom.[7] Change has also been facilitated without the need for formal enactment through the use of conventions of the constitution, rules of behaviour that have no legal force but which are adhered to by those at whom they are directed in order to make the system work.[8] They constitute the oil in the constitutional machinery. Only when the machine malfunctions or clogs up is a formal change brought about.

The constitution has endured but it has done so because of its capacity for change. The absence of any extraordinary formal means for its amendment has meant that change has been enacted through the same legislative process as that employed for enacting minor changes to the criminal and civil law of the land. The constitution stipulates a parliamentary system of government and that system makes possible change desired by any body able to command a majority in parliament, be it the crown or a political party. The principal, though not exclusive, constitutional history of the United Kingdom is to be found in the proceedings of parliament.

Through parliament, significant changes to the constitution have been achieved. In the 19th century, these included measures that fundamentally altered the relationship between the crown, parliament and the people, notably the three reform acts – the Representation of the People Acts 1832, 1867 and 1884 – and other measures covering the membership of the house of commons and outlawing corrupt practices. The century opened with a political system still heavily dominated by the crown, the ministry relying on the confidence of the monarch, and ended with a system dominated by the political party able to command a majority in the house of commons. The ministry was no longer the product of the choice of one person but the product of votes cast by several million. The 1832 act, in effect, opened the door to a democratic system.[9]

The doctrine of parliamentary supremacy – the courts being bound by the outputs of the queen-in-parliament – had been confirmed by the Glorious Revolution of 1688–9 but found its most celebrated expression through A.V. Dicey in 1885.[10] Judicial obedience to the doctrine constitutes, as H.W.R. Wade put it, 'the ultimate political fact upon

---

[5] Philip Norton, 'The Englishness of Westminster', in *These Englands*, ed. Arthur Aughey and Christine Berberich (2011).

[6] Michael Foley, *The Silence of Constitutions* (1989).

[7] See Philip Norton, 'Speaking for the People: A Conservative Narrative of Democracy', *Policy Studies* (2011).

[8] See Geoffrey Marshall, *Constitutional Conventions* (Oxford, 1984).

[9] Wicks, *The Evolution of a Constitution*, 79–80.

[10] A.V. Dicey, *An Introduction to the Study of the Law of the Constitution* (10th edn, 1959), 39–40.

which the whole system of legislation hangs'.[11] This ultimate political fact provided the basis for the now party-dominated government of the day to bring about changes to the constitutional framework of the United Kingdom, often in the face of consistent and vocal opposition. The parliamentary system has enabled the opposition to be heard but the government (usually, if determined) to get its way.

One of the most significant changes achieved by government at the beginning of the 20th century was, in many ways, the culmination of a struggle that had become marked during the closing decades of the 19th century (though predating the period, arguably by centuries), the struggle between the two Houses. The constitutional changes of the 19th century made it difficult for the house of lords to maintain a claim to be on an equal footing with the house of commons. As the earl of Shaftesbury noted during the second reading in the Lords of the 1867 Reform Bill:

> So long as the other House of Parliament was elected upon a restricted principle, I can understand that it would submit to a check from such a House as this. But in the presence of this great democratic power and the advance of this great democratic wave . . . it passes my comprehension to understand how an hereditary House like this can hold its own.[12]

The house of lords held out for another four decades before finally succumbing to the democratic wave and accepting the legislative supremacy of the elected House. The passage of the Parliament Act 1911 was a major constitutional change. By the time of its enactment, the political process in the United Kingdom was markedly different from that which had existed a century before. A century on from the 1911 act, a similar observation can be made. The British constitution in 2011 has been transformed from that which existed in 1911. This volume explores this century of change.

There is a number of generalizations that can be drawn about the nature of change that has occurred since the passage of the original Parliament Act. These encompass the extent of change, the governing party's approach to change, the contestability of change, and the form of change. A number of these challenge the accepted wisdom regarding constitutional change in the UK.

1. *The Extent of Change*

The century has seen the enactment of measures of constitutional significance which in combination have brought about change on a scale comparable to that achieved in the 19th century, if not more so. This volume examines acts of parliament which have proved to be critical in producing a shift in the relationships at the heart of the constitution. They are selected from a large number of statutes enacted. The extent of these measures can be considered by addressing them under the relationships that have been affected by their enactment.

[11] H.W.R. Wade, 'The Basis of Legal Sovereignty', *Cambridge Law Journal*, xiii (1955), 172–87, cited by E.C.S. Wade, 'Introduction', in Dicey, *An Introduction to the Study of the Law of the Constitution*, p. lvi.

[12] Hansard, *Parl. Debs*, 3rd ser., clxxxviii, cols 1925–6: 23 July 1867, quoted in Philip Norton, *The Commons in Perspective* (Oxford, 1981), 21.

1.1. *Relationship between the Two Chambers*

At the heart of the British political system is parliament. Until the passage of the Parliament Act 1911, the two chambers were formally co-equal, though the privilege of the Commons in financial matters had been conceded. The position of the Commons as the exclusive originator of taxation had been affirmed by Henry IV in 1407 and reasserted after the Restoration when a number of Lords' bills to impose taxes were denied first readings. The Commons also refused to accept the right of the Lords to amend money bills, something the Lords eventually conceded.[13] However, the Lords retained the right to reject bills, a right that was variously employed. The rejection of the budget in 1909 'until it had been submitted to the judgment of the people' triggered the assertion by the Commons of its position as the elected, and hence dominant, chamber, a dominance that the Lords formally conceded with the passage of the Parliament Bill, though as Chris Ballinger shows, it was keenly resisted and was only achieved by the willingness of the king to create new peers to ensure its passage. As Chris Ballinger also shows, the nature of the change could have been very different.

The 1911 act was the first of several measures changing the relationship between the two Houses through redefining the powers and composition of the second chamber. The first half of the century saw changes in the powers and the second half changes in the composition. In order to ensure passage of their legislation to nationalise the iron and steel industries, the Labour government of Clement Attlee achieved passage in 1949 of a second Parliament Bill to reduce the delaying power of the House over non-money bills from two sessions to one session; a measure that was itself passed under the provisions of the 1911 act.

Attention then switched from powers to composition. In order to revitalise a largely moribund House, the Conservative government of Harold Macmillan achieved passage, despite Labour opposition, of the Life Peerages Act 1958, enabling peerages to be conferred only for the lifetime of the holder (as well as permitting women to sit). The act provided the basis for a more active House, life peers proving disproportionately active in the work of the House.[14] The Peerages Act 1963, prompted by Tony Benn's campaign to disclaim his peerage (having succeeded his father as Viscount Stansgate), enabled hereditary peers to renounce their titles (and hence their place in the Lords), thus facilitating the selection that year of the earl of Home as prime minister in succession to Harold Macmillan.

An attempt to reform the composition of the House through the Parliament (No. 2) Bill in 1969 failed because of determined opposition from some Labour and Conservative back benchers, but another attempt 30 years later proved successful with the passage of the House of Lords Act 1999, removing over 600 hereditary peers from membership. The 1999 act is examined in this volume by Alexandra Kelso. The combination of the 1958 and 1999 acts served to transform the house of lords from a House dominated by Conservative hereditary peers to one comprised principally of members

---

[13] Kenneth Mackenzie, *The English Parliament* (1968), 70.
[14] Donald Shell, *The House of Lords* (Manchester, 2007), 32.

appointed on individual merit and with no one party enjoying an absolute majority. The House enjoyed, effectively, a new lease of life and demonstrated a new assertiveness.[15]

The act, however, was – like the 1911 act – seen as a temporary expedient, with later change to be enacted providing for a predominantly elected House. The period since 1999 has seen a royal commission,[16] a number of government white papers and different bodies meeting to agree proposals for reform.[17] No bill, though, was introduced by the Labour government subsequent to the 1999 act. In 2010, with the formation of a coalition government, part of the coalition agreement was to appoint a committee to draft a bill.[18] The bill was to provide – a century after the passage of the 1911 act – for a wholly, or largely elected, second chamber. The process adopted bore similarities to previous attempts to achieve reform.

1.2. *Relationship between Parliament and the People*

The 19th century saw a fundamental transformation of the relationship of parliament to the people, the demands of a burgeoning middle class – and later of artisans and workers – proving impossible to deny. The house of commons moved from being a body selected by a political elite, controlled largely by royal and aristocratic patronage, to a body elected by a majority of working men. The expansion of the franchise prompted political parties to move from being cadre to mass-membership bodies, organised in order to reach a new mass, and a new class, of electors, now too large in number to be swayed by personal contact and bribery. As Richard Crossman observed: 'organised corruption was gradually replaced by party organisation'.[19] In terms of electoral arrangements, single-member constituencies, employing the first-past-the-post method of election, became the norm.

Inequalities, though, still marked the system. There were gross disparities in the size of constituencies, the criteria for exercising the vote complex, and women were excluded from the franchise. Pressure for change, especially in the first two decades of the 20th century, resulted in further legislative change. The most prominent, but by no means the only, major measure was the Representation of the People Act 1918, discussed in this volume by Robert Blackburn. This created the basis for the electoral system that has endured since. It not only reformed the electoral system and simplified the franchise, but also extended the vote to women aged 30 years and over. The same year another act enabled women aged 21 years and over to stand for election to parliament.

As Robert Blackburn explains, the act created the framework for the electoral system but failed to resolve the question of the system of election to be employed. The issue of electoral reform has remained on the agenda ever since, with various attempts to introduce the alternative vote (AV) or a system of proportional representation (PR). An

---

[15] See Meg Russell, 'A Stronger Second Chamber? Assessing the Impact of House of Lords Reform in 1999 and the Lessons for Bicameralism', *Political Studies*, lviii (2010).

[16] Royal Commission on the Reform of the House of Lords, *A House for the Future*, Cm. 4534 (2000).

[17] For a summary, see Philip Norton, 'The House of Lords', in *Politics UK*, ed. Bill Jones and Philip Norton (7th edn, 2010), 368–70.

[18] HM Government, *The Coalition: Our Programme for Government* (2010), 27. It was subsequently announced that the bill would be subject to pre-legislative scrutiny.

[19] Richard Crossman, 'Introduction', in Walter Bagehot, *The English Constitution* (1963), 39.

attempt to introduce the AV in 1931 floundered because of opposition in the house of lords. In 1998 a report from the Independent Commission on the Electoral System (the Jenkins Commission) recommended the use of the alternative vote plus (AV+) for parliamentary elections. In 2010 the coalition government agreed to introduce a bill providing for a referendum on whether the AV should replace the first-past-the-post system. The issue throughout the century has been divisive between, as well as within, political parties. While the method of electing MPs has been that of first past the post (exclusively so following the abolition of university seats in 1950, some of which employed the single transferable vote), other methods have been introduced for electing members of other bodies in the period since 1997. The European parliament, the devolved assemblies, the mayor and members of the Greater London Assembly and Scottish local government utilise different electoral systems.[20]

The 1918 act has been supplemented by later measures.[21] The People (Equal Franchise) Act 1928 equalised the voting age for men and women. Later acts in 1944, 1945 and 1947 resulted in the creation of a permanent Boundary Commission, assimilated local government and parliamentary franchises, and made changes to the rules governing boundary reviews. The Representation of the People Act 1948 made further significant changes, including abolishing plural voting, university seats and two-member seats. Other measures since have included the Representation of the People Act 1969, the Representation of the People Act 1983, the Political Parties, Elections and Referendums Act 2000, the Electoral Administration Act 2006 and the Political Parties and Elections Act 2009. The 1969 act lowered the voting age to 18 years and the 2006 act lowered the age at which one could stand for election to public office similarly to 18 years.

In 2010 the coalition government also sought further major change by introducing a measure, the Parliamentary Voting System and Constituencies Bill, to reduce the size of the house of commons and equalise constituency boundaries (as well as hold a referendum on AV). Though the number of seats in the House had been reduced following the loss of Irish seats in 1922, only one significant reduction in the number of seats has been legislated for during the century since 1911. Following devolution, there was a reduction in the number of seats in Scotland from 72 to 59. The coalition also introduced a Fixed-term Parliaments Bill, a major constitutional innovation limiting the prerogative as to when an election could be called. The Parliament Act 1911 had amended the Septennial Act 1716 to reduce the maximum length of a parliament from seven to five years, but within that period a prime minister could request the sovereign to grant a dissolution. The bill introduced by the coalition provided that a premature election could take place only if voted for by a two-thirds majority of all MPs or if a new ministry could not be formed within 14 days of a government losing a vote of confidence.

One other aspect of the relationship between parliament and people that changed was the willingness of parliament to refer matters to the people through the medium of a referendum. Calls for the use of referendums had variously been made in the first half of the 20th century and indeed earlier. Liberal Unionists had advocated one in the 1890s

---

[20] See Ministry of Justice, *Review of Voting Systems: The Experience of New Voting Systems in the United Kingdom Since 1997*, Cm. 7304 (2008).

[21] See Robert Blackburn, *The Electoral System in Britain* (Basingstoke, 1995), *passim*.

on the issue of Irish home rule. Joseph Chamberlain, early in the new century, advocated one on tariff reform and in 1910 the Conservative (then known as the Unionist) Party committed itself to referendums for resolving major constitutional disputes. Later Conservative leaders, Stanley Baldwin and Winston Churchill, raised the possibility of referendums on protection and the continuation of the wartime coalition respectively. Although referendums were variously sanctioned at local or sub-national level (as in Northern Ireland in 1973), it was not until 1975 that the first UK-wide referendum, on continued membership of the European Community (EC), was held.

Referendums at sub-UK level have since been held in respect of devolution to Scotland, Wales, Northern Ireland and London (that in Northern Ireland having a broader constitutional reach) and UK-wide referendums promised in the event of government agreeing particular measures (as on a single European currency). In 2010, as already noted, the coalition government introduced a bill to provide for a referendum on the introduction of the AV. The referendums have been advisory (though it would be perverse for parliament to authorise one and then ignore the result), but none the less raise questions about the legitimacy of outcomes not authorised by referendum, especially salient in the context of an uncodified constitution.[22]

1.3. *Relationship between the State and the Individual*

The rights of the individual in relation to the state have historically been viewed as negative, or residual, that is, an individual has the right to do whatever he or she wishes so long as it is not in violation of the law of the land. Individual liberty has been secured by judicial decisions determining the rights of individuals in cases brought before the courts.[23] As F.A. Mann observed in 1978: 'Such human rights as the law of this country recognises are almost entirely judge-made and in many instances involve no more than a rebuttal presumption to the effect that Parliament is unlikely to have intended to interfere with or destroy them.'[24] Such assumptions about parliament largely dominated for much of the century. Parliament was seen as part of the solution, standing ready to protect the individual against the state, rather than as part of the problem, being willing to enact measures that eroded the rights of the individual.[25]

However, such attitudes were challenged in the latter half of the 20th century. War-time demonstrated the capacity of parliament to enact major measures imposing state control over citizens. Many of these powers were ended in peacetime, but a number of politicians and jurists queried the extent to which parliament was able to protect (either by positive action or by refusing to limit) the liberties of the individual. As government extended its legislative reach more and more into the public sphere, with parliament willingly enacting its measures, some began to advocate a bill of rights, enumerating in legislative form a code of human rights. An entrenched bill of rights

---

[22] On the arguments for and against referendums, see House of Lords Select Committee on the Constitution, *Referendums in the United Kingdom*, 12th Report of Session 2009–10, HL Paper 99 (2010).

[23] Eric Barendt, *An Introduction to Constitutional Law* (Oxford, 1998), 46–7.

[24] F.A. Mann, 'Britain's Bill of Rights', *Law Quarterly Review*, xciv (1978), 514.

[25] See, e.g., Ronald Butt, *The Power of Parliament* (1967), 437.

would put the rights of the individual beyond the control of a transient majority in the house of commons; even without entrenchment, enumerating the rights in statute would enable the courts to provide greater protection than possible under the common law.

Demands for such a bill of rights became prominent in the 1960s – Anthony Lester's Fabian Society Tract, *Democracy and Individual Rights*, was published in 1968 and was followed by other campaigning pamphlets. In the 1976 Dimbleby Lecture, Lord Hailsham attacked what he termed the 'elective dictatorship' that now characterised British government and advocated a written constitution and a bill of rights.[26] Though Labour politicians were initially wary of such demands – fearing a bill of rights could limit the radical policies of a Labour government – the party leadership came round to the view that some form of statutory protection was justified. Under the leadership of Neil Kinnock, it moved to favour a charter of rights but later under the leadership of John Smith embraced the incorporation of the European Convention for the Protection of Human Rights and Fundamental Freedoms – commonly referred to as the European Convention on Human Rights (ECHR)[27] – into UK law, a commitment maintained by Tony Blair.

The promulgation in 1950 of the ECHR, to which Britain had contributed and was to be an early signatory, was seen initially as for other countries – for 'lesser breeds without the law'[28] – but, as Peter Mandelson and Roger Liddle wrote in 1996, in *The Blair Revolution*: 'Infringements of basic rights in Britain now force a rethink.'[29] The Labour manifesto in the 1997 general election declared: 'Citizens should have statutory rights to enforce their human rights in the UK courts. We will by statute incorporate the European Convention on Human Rights into UK law to bring these rights home and allow our people access to them in their national courts.'[30] The result was the Human Rights Bill introduced in the first session of the new parliament.

The Human Rights Act 1998 is discussed in detail in this volume by David Feldman. The act was crafted in order not to challenge the doctrine of parliamentary sovereignty, but added fundamentally to the new juridical dimension to the British constitution. It created a challenge both for courts and the executive, the former in being trained in the interpretation of such a document and the latter in being willing to accept declarations of incompatibility by the courts. Though ministers have accepted such declarations, it has not always been with a good grace.[31] Parliament for its part has sought to ensure that government complies with the act and established a joint committee on human rights.[32] David Feldman served as the first legal adviser to the committee.

---

[26] Lord Hailsham, *Elective Dictatorship* (1976).

[27] On the convention, see A.H. Robertson and J.G. Merrills, *Human Rights in Europe* (3rd edn, Manchester, 1993).

[28] Peter Mandelson and Roger Liddle, *The Blair Revolution: Can New Labour Deliver?* (1996), 193.

[29] Mandelson and Liddle, *The Blair Revolution*, 194.

[30] The Labour Party, *New Labour: Because Britain Deserves Better* (1997), 35.

[31] See Philip Norton, 'The Constitution: Selective Incrementalism Continues', in *The Palgrave Review of British Politics 2005*, ed. M. Rush and P. Giddings (Basingstoke, 2006), 16–18.

[32] Philip Norton, 'Parliament and Human Rights', in *An Era of Human Rights*, ed. D. Ryland (Patrington, 2006), 375–94.

1.4. *Relationship between the UK and the Rest of the World*

The 20th century began with the British empire being a major, if not the major, world force. The writ of the queen empress covered approximately one-fifth of the globe. Parliament could, and did, legislate for countries other than those within the British Isles. The first half of the century saw the transition from empire to a much looser (but still significant) Commonwealth of Nations and the end of the century witnessed Britain seeking to regain a role on the world stage through membership of the EC.

The transition was not always peaceful, including within the British Isles. Irish home rule bedevilled British politics at the end of the 19th century and the beginning of the 20th. What was later to be known as the West Lothian, or English, question in the debates on devolution in the 1970s and since – how to cope with the asymmetrical relationship between members from the central and the devolved parliaments – was a feature of that debate.[33] The Irish uprising forced the UK government to recognize Irish demands for self-determination. The Government of Ireland Act 1920 granted home rule and divided the country into two. The provisions governing the south proved stillborn with the continuing conflict leading to the Treaty of Ireland in 1922. The writ of parliament ceased to run in Eire.

Its writ also later ceased to run in much of the empire. The Statute of Westminster 1931 removed limitations on the competence of dominion parliaments and provided that no act of parliament passed subsequent to the act should be part of the law of a dominion: 'unless it is expressly declared in that Act that that Dominion has requested, and consented to, the enactment thereof'.[34] Later measures were enacted to give greater powers of self-determination and later still to transfer sovereign authority to countries that had been granted independence. Some of these measures were hotly contested, Winston Churchill being to the fore in opposing the Government of India Bill in 1935, but they made it to the statute book, essentially as a means of enacting what governments recognized as inevitable, even if that was not the view taken by all their back benchers.

The loss of empire created a conundrum for British governments in determining what role the United Kingdom could and should play on the world stage. Dean Acheson's observation that Britain had lost an empire but had yet to find a role has been much quoted. The failure of the Commonwealth to provide the political base, and trading partner, that the UK may have hoped for, and the failure of the Suez expedition in 1956, exacerbated the conundrum. In the event, another medium for British engagement on the international stage was found. Having initially resisted calls to be involved in the process of their formation, the UK government decided to apply for membership of the EC. The decision was made by the Conservative government of Harold Macmillan, though it was not until 1972, under the premiership of Edward Heath, that the terms of membership were agreed. The United Kingdom became a member of the EC on 1 January 1973. The constitutional implications were profound, requiring a major adaptation of existing constitutional norms. The European Communities Act 1972, providing the basis in UK law for membership, is treated in this volume. Membership entailed a

[33] See Norton, 'The Englishness of Westminster'.
[34] Statute of Westminster 1931, section 4.

supranational body being able to craft law that was to apply within the United Kingdom, the assent of parliament having been given in advance under the terms of the 1972 act; UK law was to be construed as far as possible to be compatible with EC law, and in the event of a perceived conflict the issue was to be resolved by the courts and EC law was to take precedence. It was seen by critics as undermining the doctrine of parliamentary sovereignty. The courts could strike down provisions of UK law if contrary to the treaties or EC law. The act thus created a new juridical dimension to the British constitution, conferring on the courts a role they had not performed since before the Glorious Revolution of 1688.

The 1972 act was to be complemented by others, giving effect to new treaties that further altered the relationship between member states and the institutions of the EC, later (under the Maastricht Treaty) the European Union (EU). The treaties were contested, the government having particular difficulty in achieving passage of the European Communities Bill in 1972 and the European Communities (Amendment) Bill in 1992–3, on each occasion having to resort to votes of confidence in order to ensure their passage.[35]

1.5. *Relationship between the Centre and the Rest of the United Kingdom*

The British government, during the course of the century, not only had to adjust to new relationships with other nations beyond the UK's shores, it also had to adjust to new relationships within the British Isles. Demands for home rule for Scotland and Wales were made by the Scottish National Party (SNP) and Plaid Cymru (PC) respectively but their principal success until the 1960s was simply to survive. In the 1960s they began to make some political gains. In Northern Ireland, the Nationalist Party, Sinn Fein, pressed for unification with Eire and in the late 1960s demands for civil rights for Roman catholics in the province led to conflict. In 1971 a shooting war broke out between the Irish Republican Army (IRA), the military wing of Sinn Fein, and the British army.

A royal commission on the constitution in 1973 recommended devolution to Scotland and Wales.[36] Recognizing the political threat from the SNP in its own political power-base of Scotland, the Labour Party came to embrace devolution and in the 1974–9 parliament achieved passage of the Scotland Act 1978 and the Wales Act 1978; however, MPs had insisted on referendums in both cases as well as imposing a threshold for a 'yes' vote to take effect. The electorate in Wales voted 'no' and in Scotland the threshold was (narrowly) missed. Successive governments sought to resolve the troubles in Northern Ireland.

The return of a Labour government in 1997 heralded another attempt to achieve devolution, this time successfully. Referendums were held in Scotland and Wales, achieving a clear 'yes' vote in Scotland and a narrow 'yes' vote in Wales. Parliament enacted the Scotland Act 1998 and the Government of Wales Act 1998, devolving executive and

[35] Though on the Treaty of Lisbon, see Philip Cowley and Mark Stuart, 'Where has all the Trouble Gone? British Intra-party Parliamentary Divisions during the Lisbon Ratification', *British Politics*, v (2010), 136.

[36] *Royal Commission on the Constitution 1969–1973, Vol. 1: Report*, Cmnd. 5460 (1973).

legislative powers to a Scottish parliament and executive powers to a National Assembly for Wales. Barry Winetrobe examines the Scotland Act in this volume.

Separately, attempts to achieve peace in Northern Ireland resulted in the Good Friday agreement, the endorsement of that agreement in referendums in Northern Ireland and the Republic of Ireland, and the creation of a Northern Ireland Assembly. After the Assembly was twice suspended, agreement was reached in 2007 and, following new elections, a power-sharing government was formed between the parties on the two extremes of the political spectrum, the Democratic Unionists and Sinn Fein. Despite some continuing tensions, the unique political arrangement in the province – ministerial posts allocated according to party strength, no use of the concept of collective responsibility, and the posts of first minister and deputy first minister essentially constituting conjoined posts – has endured.

The United Kingdom has thus acquired a significant level of government between the national and local level. Three of the four parts of the union have an elected legislature. The absence of an English parliament has led to calls for such a parliament and, in the absence of such a body, for the West Lothian, or English, question to be addressed.[37] There have also been calls for a further strengthening of the devolved bodies. The Government of Wales Act 2006 provided the basis for the transfer of certain legislative powers and the holding of a referendum for a more comprehensive transfer. In 2009, the Commission on Scottish Devolution (the Calman Commission) made various recommendations, especially in respect of strengthening communication and co-operation between Westminster and Holyrood.[38] The issue of devolution, and its consequences for the UK parliament, remain politically salient.

What is clear from this brief overview is the sheer extent of constitutional change to have taken place during the century since the passage of the Parliament Act in 1911. The overview is far from comprehensive and does not exhaust the relationships that exist at the heart of the British constitution. Over the century, the relationship between crown and people has changed substantially, the most traumatic dislocation – the decision of Edward VIII to give up the throne – requiring legislative authority (His Majesty's Declaration of Abdication Act 1936); other acts have dealt with royal titles and the provisions governing a regency. There have also been some changes in the relationship between Church and state in respect of the established Church, the Church of England. The Church of England Assembly (Powers) Act 1919 provided the process for parliamentary approval of Church of England measures. Over the century, the significance of crown and Church as political actors declined in the face of the other developments enhancing the power of the executive.

The extent of change has, thus, been substantial. That is clear from the foregoing. What is less obvious from the foregoing, but may be gleaned from the specific measures selected for inclusion in this volume, is the difference between those measures enacted prior to 1997 and those enacted since. There has been a notable difference in approach taken by governments to constitutional change, affecting both the nature and extent of change.

---

[37] Norton, 'The Englishness of Westminster'.

[38] Commission on Scottish Devolution, *Serving Scotland Better: Scotland and the United Kingdom in the 21st Century*, Final Report (Edinburgh, 2009).

2. The Governing Party's Approach to Change

There is a discernible difference between pre- and post-1997 governments as to the approach taken to constitutional change. 'Traditionally', wrote Robert Stevens, 'the growth of the English Constitution has been organic; the rate of change glacial.'[39] Until recent times, there was, he said, one possible exception: the period from 1640 to around 1720. There have been major constitutional changes since, but 'they were essentially independent acts rather than part of a dramatic period of constitutional restructuring'.[40]

That this should be so is not surprising. For much of the 20th century, the constitution was not viewed as a matter of political contention. Any changes were viewed as adjustments, made necessary by a perceived failing of a particular part of the constitutional framework. There was no clear conception of the state, with political power being seen in personalised terms through the medium of the crown, a consequence of the longevity of the constitution.[41] There was, thus, little experience of, or inclination toward, discussing the constitution in conceptual terms, that is, the constitution *qua* constitution.

The stance towards constitutional change was, thus, reactive. There was no questioning of the fundamentals of the basic constitutional framework. The constitution was under-pinned by prescription; it had endured and been proved by time. It was seen as a balanced constitution, able to adjust to the needs of the time; the changes that took place were seen as evidence of the versatility of the constitution.[42] In so far as it was mentioned, it was for the purpose of praise or emulation. In 1967, Karl Loewenstein referred to its 'proven usefulness and practicality'.[43] The constitution provided the framework within which government could govern – maintaining the balance between raising resources to fulfil commitments of public policy and the consent of the people.

It was only when the constitutional framework seemed inadequate to meet popular expectations that demands for change grew and different approaches to constitutional change began to emerge. In the last three decades of the 20th century, the consensus fragmented and several intellectually-coherent approaches to constitutional change developed, each positing a different constitutional framework as most appropriate to the United Kingdom.[44] It is possible to identify seven such approaches,[45] though by the end of the century debate crystallised around two of them – the liberal and the traditional. The liberal approach embraced the concept of negative constitutionalism,[46] viewing the constitution as a medium of constraint, fragmenting political power and placing fundamental values beyond the reach of simple majorities in the two houses of parliament. The traditional approach supported the dominant Westminster system, viewing it as melding,

[39] Robert Stevens, *The English Judges* (Oxford, 2002), p. xiii.

[40] Stevens, *The English Judges*, p. xiii.

[41] Tony Prosser, 'Understanding the British Constitution', in *Constitutionalism in Transformation: European and Theoretical Perspectives*, ed. Richard Bellamy and Dario Castiglione (Oxford, 1996), 61–75.

[42] Norton, *The Constitution in Flux*, 23.

[43] Karl Loewenstein, *British Cabinet Government* (Oxford, 1967), 6.

[44] Norton, *The Constitution in Flux*, 261–94.

[45] Philip Norton, 'The Constitution: Approaches to Reform', *Politics Review*, iii (1993), 2–5.

[46] See Duncan Ivison, 'Pluralism and the Hobbesian Logic of Negative Constitutionalism', *Political Studies*, xlvii (1999), 83–99.

in a way no other system could, popular will (positive constitutionalism) and the tempering effects of parliament. The liberal approach, championed by the constitutional reform movement Charter '88 (formed in the tercentenary year of the Glorious Revolution), tended to make the running in debate.

The demands for change influenced thinking in the Labour Party. Under Michael Foot, it had adopted a socialist approach to constitutional change, reflected in its manifesto for the 1983 general election. This was abandoned under the leadership of Neil Kinnock and John Smith. Smith came to embrace much of the Charter '88 agenda.[47] His reform agenda was continued under the leadership of Tony Blair. The result was a manifesto in the 1997 general election committing the party to a package of measures of constitutional reform, in particular devolution, the incorporation of the ECHR into domestic law, reform of the house of lords, and an independent commission to propose an alternative electoral system to that of first past the post.

The governing party's approach thus switched from being reactive to being proactive. The first two sessions of the parliament saw an emphasis on measures of major constitutional reform, three of those measures (Human Rights Act, Scotland Act, House of Lords Act) being treated in this volume. There was also a later measure in the form of the Constitutional Reform Act 2005, creating a supreme court for the United Kingdom and removing the lord chancellor as head of the judiciary. The measures were significant both individually and collectively. Indeed, Robert Stevens saw the period as on a par with the period from 1640 to 1720. Taken with the European Communities Act, the period was exceptional. 'For lawyers and the courts', he wrote, 'the period from 1970 to 2000 provided a practical and psychological transformation comparable with the earlier constitutional revolution.'[48]

The changes brought about by the Labour government of Tony Blair (1997–2007) were substantial, in combination altering significantly the contours of the British constitution.[49] 'The reign of Dicey', wrote Stevens, 'was coming, relatively peacefully, to a close.'[50] However, there was one comment by Stevens that suggested an element of continuity: the commitments made by John Smith, he said, were to have a profound impact on the future of the judiciary, but 'they lacked coherence'.[51] Labour was persuaded of the case for change but advocated each measure essentially on its own merits. There was no clear constitutional theory underpinning the approach. Tony Blair presided over a period of constitutional change but took notably little interest in the subject and had no defined or clearly-articulated view of the constitution he deemed appropriate for the United Kingdom.[52] It was left largely to the lord chancellor, Lord Irvine of Lairg, who in 2002 admitted that the government had no overarching theory; it proceeded, he said, 'by way of pragmatism based on principle'.[53] He enunciated three principles:

[47] Mark Stuart, *John Smith: A Life* (2005), 293–5.

[48] Stevens, *The English Judges*, p. xiii.

[49] See, e.g., Dawn Oliver, *Constitutional Reform in the UK* (Oxford, 2003); Anthony King, *The British Constitution* (Oxford, 2007); Vernon Bogdanor, *The New British Constitution* (Oxford, 2009).

[50] Stevens, *The English Judges*, p. xiv.

[51] Stevens, *The English Judges*, p. xiv.

[52] Philip Norton, 'The Constitution', in *Blair's Britain 1997–2007*, ed. Anthony Seldon (Cambridge, 2007), 121; Philip Norton, 'Tony Blair and the Constitution', *British Politics*, ii (2007), 269–81.

[53] Hansard, *Lords Debates*, 5th ser., dcxlii, col. 691: 18 Dec. 2002.

The first is that we should remain a parliamentary democracy with the Westminster Parliament supreme and within that the other place the dominant partner. Secondly . . . we should increase public engagement in democracy, developing a mature democracy with different centres of power where individuals enjoy greater rights and where government is carried out closer to the people . . . Our third principle is that the correct road to reform was to devise a solution to each problem on its own terms.[54]

The first two of these were not obviously compatible in locating political power in the United Kingdom and the third was not so much a principle as an escape clause. The incoherence was reflected in conflict in respect of devolution, the prime minister wanting to have devolution but still control outcomes from Downing Street. The commitment to establish a commission on the voting system was carried out, but not the commitment then to hold a referendum on the electoral system. There was no change to first past the post as the method of electing MPs. Following some of the judgments of the courts in applying the Human Rights Act, some ministers objected bitterly to the actions of the judges and the prime minister warned of changes to the act.

There was, thus, continuity in that change proceeded from no intellectually-coherent approach to constitutional change. The constitutional framework was being changed but without a clear view of the type of constitution that was being created.[55] The government's measures moved some way towards the liberal view of the constitution but stopped considerably short of the agenda embraced by that approach.

A similar lack of an intellectually-coherent approach was to be found when a coalition government was formed in 2010. The Conservative opposition in the period from 1997 to 2010 generally had no problem in determining its stance on the measures introduced by the Labour government. Embracing essentially the traditional approach, it opposed substantial change to the extant constitution. However, it faced a problem prospectively, in that when it returned to office the constitution would no longer be that which it had been defending when it was in power. It could, therefore, adopt a reactionary, conservative or radical approach.[56] In practice, it devoted little time to considering the issue and its 2010 manifesto could be described as adopting a conservative approach with a radical tinge.[57] It favoured a British bill of rights in place of the Human Rights Act, having MPs from English seats only vote on English-only legislation, and seeking a consensus in moving towards a largely-elected house of lords, though party leader, David Cameron, had said the last of these was essentially a 'third-term issue'.

The uncertain outcome of the 2010 general election and the creation of a coalition government altered the approach taken. The parties to the coalition represented diametrically-opposed approaches. The coalition adopted the underlying liberal thesis that 'our political system is broken'[58] – the traditional view is that it is fundamentally sound – and agreed a series of measures that, like the previous government, adhered to no clear approach to constitutional change. As we have seen, the changes embraced a

---

[54] Hansard, *Lords Debates*, 5th ser., dcxlii, col. 692: 18 Dec. 2002.

[55] See Sir John Baker, 'Our Unwritten Constitution', *Proceedings of the British Academy*, clxvii (2010), 91–117.

[56] Philip Norton, 'The Constitution', in *The Political Thought of the Conservative Party Since 1945*, ed. Kevin Hickson (Basingstoke, 2005), 106–9.

[57] Norton, 'Speaking for the People'.

[58] HM Government, *The Coalition: Our Programme for Government*, 26.

referendum on the AV (not going far enough for the liberal approach and too far for the traditional) and the introduction of fixed-term parliaments, as well as the introduction of a Freedom Bill, the creation of a mainly or wholly elected second chamber on the basis of PR, a reduction in the number of MPs and commissions to examine the West Lothian question and the case for a British bill of rights.

There was, thus, the prospect of a third era of major constitutional reform – the government adopting a proactive rather than a reactive stance – but with the same feature of continuity, that is, the absence of any intellectually-coherent approach to constitutional change. The coalition was dominated by a party that adhered essentially to the traditional approach but was pursuing a political agenda that embraced significant elements of the liberal approach. The capacity for conflict between, and within, parties, as with previous measures of constitutional reform, was all too apparent and began to show within weeks of the coalition being formed.

3. *The Contestability of Change*

It is not unusual for governments to seek some measure of cross-party agreement in order to implement changes to the constitution. On occasion, Speaker's conferences, commissions or cross-party gatherings may be held. There is an obvious attraction to be able to move forward on changes to the nation's constitutional framework with the consent of most, or the main, political parties and not just the party that temporarily holds the reins of power. As the contributions to the volume show, there have been Speaker's conferences to address changes to electoral practices and cross-party conferences or meetings to address reform of the house of lords.

In practice, however, consensus is rare. Measures are usually introduced without the support of the opposition and, even where there has been some measure of cross-party agreement it is no guarantee that the measure will not be contested or not even a guarantee that it will make it to the statute book. The Parliament (No. 2) Bill introduced in 1968 enjoyed cross-party support. It had been preceded by cross-party talks (though aborted) and by a white paper.[59] Despite government and opposition support for the white paper, a back-bench amendment to reject it garnered 159 votes.[60] The bill received a second reading by 285 votes to 135,[61] again despite opposition advice to support it. The government failed to impose a guillotine and opponents kept the House sitting late on amendments and variously dividing on them as well as on closure motions.[62] Eventually, the government had problems keeping enough of its MPs present to carry closure motions and decided not to proceed with the bill.[63]

The Parliament (No. 2) Bill was unusual in being lost, though on other occasions governments may be wary of bringing measures forward if they anticipate strong opposi-

---

[59] Janet Morgan, *The House of Lords and the Labour Government 1964–1970* (Oxford 1975), 169–94.

[60] The amendment was lost by 270 votes to 159. Hansard, *Commons Debates,* 6th ser., dcclxxiii, cols 1429–34: 20 Nov. 1968; Philip Norton, *Dissension in the House of Commons 1945–74* (Basingstoke, 1975), 304–5.

[61] Hansard, *Commons Debates,* 5th ser., dcclxxvii, cols 167–72: 3 Feb. 1969.

[62] See Norton, *Dissension in the House of Commons 1945–74*, pp. 317–54, *passim.*

[63] Morgan, *The House of Lords and the Labour Government 1964–1970*, pp. 216–8.

tion. Though the Labour government variously sought support for a further reform of the house of lords following passage of the House of Lords Act 1999, it never introduced a bill. Where governments have proceeded with significant measures of constitutional reform, they have normally done so in the teeth of opposition, be it from the official opposition and/or dissident back benchers. Of the measures covered in this volume, only one – the Representation of the People Act 1918 – was, as Robert Blackburn shows, the product of cross-party consensus. The rest were contested, requiring, in some cases, extraordinary action by government to ensure their passage. In the case of the Parliament Bill, the agreement of the monarch to create new peers was necessary to overcome resistance in the house of lords and in 1972 Prime Minister Edward Heath resorted to a vote of confidence to ensure a second reading of the European Communities Bill. In 1999, as Alexandra Kelso shows, the government agreed to the Weatherill amendment, to retain 92 hereditary peers, in order to smooth passage of the House of Lords Bill and avoid peers also causing problems with other parts of the government's programme for the session.

The measures, then, have generally been demonstrably the product of a particular government. Changes to the constitution have, thus, taken place on essentially a partisan, certainly a politically-contested, basis. The adversarial nature of the British political system encourages opposition to oppose such measures, especially if they see political mileage in so doing. The result may be – as with the European Communities Bill – that opposition MPs vote against a measure that they may in principle support.

4. *The Form of Change*

One other feature that is apparent from the contributions to this study is that major constitutional change is not necessarily achieved through the medium of big bills. Some of the bills examined in this volume are notable for their brevity. This may reflect the fact that only one substantive change is involved. The House of Lords Bill in 1999 was initially little more than a one-clause bill, excluding hereditary peers from the house of lords. It may also be the product of political expediency. The devolution legislation was drafted in the light of experience of the 1970s, when the Scotland and Wales Bills stipulated powers that were to be devolved. The Scotland Bill in 1998 instead simply listed those matters that were to be reserved to Westminster. In drafting the European Communities Bill in 1972, a decision had to be taken as to whether to employ a one-clause enabling bill or a gargantuan bill listing all legislation to be amended as a consequence of membership. As we detail in the study of the bill, the government essentially opted for the former. There is a tendency on the part of government to want to balance the right of parliament to discuss thoroughly a measure of constitutional reform with its wish to get it enacted, along with other measures, in the session. Measures of constitutional reform have, thus, been produced not only to meet the drafting requirements of parliamentary counsel but also to meet the political needs of government.

5. *Consequences*

Each of the contributors to the volume addresses not only the passage of the bill through parliament but also the consequences of the measure. The measures generally have the intended effect – limiting the power of the second chamber, for example, or enabling the UK to become a member of the EC. However, they may also have wider and unintended adverse, or unanticipated, effects.

Some measures have not had the effects predicted by critics. The extension of the franchise to women in 1918 did not produce eccentric voting behaviour or propel the Conservative Party to the political wilderness. The house of lords was not weakened in its capacity to influence government by the passage of the House of Lords Act 1999. If anything, the House was to bear out claims of the leader of the House, Baroness Jay, that it was more legitimate and proved willing to defeat the government on a range of issues, not least civil liberties.[64]

Critics of the European Communities Bill, on the other hand, have grounds for believing that some of their claims as to the constitutional implications of membership of the EC were more accurate than those of government, ministers dismissing claims that parliamentary sovereignty would be undermined and claiming that little subordinate legislation would be necessary to give effect to EC obligations. The Human Rights Act 1998 resulted in some cases that provided succour for critics of the act – though the number of cases involving declarations of incompatibility has been small – and produced criticism, sometimes in quite stark terms, from within the ranks of the government, including Downing Street. Prime Minister Tony Blair had to be persuaded that amendment of the act was not necessary.

The consequences of measures of constitutional reform were, therefore, not certain, though in this respect they differ little from other legislation and, like all acts, were not subject to post-legislative scrutiny. Constitutional measures were left to take effect, their impact to be assessed by scholars and commentators. Only in 2008 did the government accept the case for post-legislative review by departments of acts three to five years after enactment, the reviews to be submitted to the relevant select committees in the house of commons. The first act of constitutional significance to be subject to such review was the Constitutional Reform Act 2005.[65]

There are, though, two generalizations that can be drawn under this heading from the studies in this volume. One is that parliament has proved capable of adapting its own procedures to cope with constitutional change. This has proved most obviously the case in respect of membership of the EC (now the EU) and the enactment of the Human Rights Act, both Houses creating committees to examine European documents and jointly the committee on human rights. There is a highly-institutionalised process of parliamentary scrutiny,[66] in essence drawing on the complementary nature of the two chambers that is not achieved in any other area.

The other is that the acts did not still debate. Each may have been an event but was also part of a process. As Robert Blackburn shows, debate about the electoral system

---

[64] Meg Russell and Maria Sciara, 'The Policy Impact of Defeats in the House of Lords', *British Journal of Politics and International Relations*, x (2008), 571–89.

[65] *Memorandum to the Justice Select Committee: Post-legislative Assessment of the Constitutional Reform Act 2005*, Cm. 7814 (2010).

[66] See Philip Norton, 'The United Kingdom: Political Conflict, Parliamentary Scrutiny', in *National Parliaments and the European Union*, ed. Philip Norton (1996), 92–109; David Feldman, 'Parliamentary Scrutiny of Legislation and Human Rights, *Public Law* (2002), 323–48; Carolyn Evans, 'Legislative Scrutiny Committees and Parliamentary Conceptions of Human Rights', *Public Law* (2006), 785–806.

continues. The issue of the second chamber remains current. There are demands for more powers to be devolved to the different parts of the United Kingdom and for the creation of an English parliament; the issues of 'English votes on English Bills' and the Barnett formula remain current.[67] The coalition government formed in 2010, as we have seen, is exploring the possibility of an English bill of rights to supersede the Human Rights Act.

That this debate should be taking place is not that surprising, given the complex nature of the British constitution – militating against discrete change to any particular part – and the fragmentation of the previous consensus. What was once a settled constitution is now far from settled, recent governments having set out to reshape the constitutional landscape but without any clear conception of what the final shape should or will be.[68] New pieces of the constitutional jigsaw have been brought into play. What remains missing is the box lid.

---

[67] On the latter, see House of Lords Select Committee on the Barnett Formula, *The Barnett Formula*, 1st Report of Session 2008–09, HL Paper 139 (2009).

[68] See Norton, 'Tony Blair and the Constitution', 280; Baker, 'Our Unwritten Constitution', 92; King, *The British Constitution*, 345–54.

Hedging and Ditching: The Parliament Act 1911

CHRIS BALLINGER

The Parliament Act 1911 is a short act of parliament, which had a profound effect on constitutional and political legislation in the 20th century. The purpose of the Parliament Act was very clear: to limit the power of the house of lords to impede the programme of a government with a majority in the house of commons. The act achieved this by introducing three innovations: (1) it put on the statute book the primacy of the house of commons over financial legislation; (2) the house of lords' absolute veto over legislation in most areas was replaced by a suspensory veto of approximately two years; (3) the act reduced the maximum duration of a parliament from seven years to five. But at the start of the parliament, in 1906, it was not clear that this programme would prevail: its enactment over alternative proposals was helped by a combination of the leadership of Campbell-Bannerman and Asquith, political conflict, electoral and parliamentary arithmetic, and the politics of the Irish question. The Parliament Act fundamentally and irreconcilably altered the legislative process in the United Kingdom, whilst arguably leaving the *de facto* constitutional position unchanged. In doing so, it facilitated a century of constitutional legislation.

Keywords: Parliament Act; Irish home rule; people's budget 1909; Finance Bill 1909; house of commons; house of lords; general elections: January 1910; December 1910; Sir Henry Campbell-Bannerman (prime minister); H.H. Asquith (prime minister); King George V; hedgers and ditchers; suspensory veto

1. *Overview*

The Parliament Act 1911 is a short act of parliament, which had a profound effect on constitutional and political legislation in the 20th century. The purpose of the Parliament Act was very clear: to limit the power of the house of lords to impede the programme of a government with a majority in the house of commons. The act itself did three things. First, it put on the statute book the primacy of the house of commons over financial legislation by limiting to one month the Lords' power of delay over money bills.[1] Second, the house of lords' absolute veto over legislation (apart from financial provisions or legislation to extend the duration of a parliament) was replaced by a suspensory veto of approximately two years. Third, the act reduced the maximum duration of a parliament from seven years to five. The Parliament Act fundamentally, and irreconcilably, altered the legislative process in the United Kingdom, whilst arguably

---

[1] Jaconelli cites this as a rare instance of turning a constitutional convention into a statutory provision, referencing the Statute of Westminster 1931 as a better-known example. J. Jaconelli, 'The Parliament Bill 1910–1911: The Mechanics of Constitutional Protection', *Parliamentary History*, x (1991), 280.

leaving the *de facto* constitutional position unchanged. And what seemed to some to be a temporary expedient – unfinished business[2] – was to prevail for a century.

2. *Why was the Bill Introduced?*

2.1. *What was the Context?*

2.1.1. Commons and Lords 1906–9

The landslide Liberal election victory of 1906 had given Sir Henry Campbell-Bannerman's government 400 seats in the house of commons; the Unionists had just 157. In the house of lords, however, only 88 of the 602 members were identified as Liberals. With the government committed to a radical programme of social and constitutional reform, it seemed likely from the outset that some conflict between Commons and Lords would occur. But in the election campaign itself, Liberal candidates rarely discussed the powers of the Lords. The scale of the election victory, and the controversy that surrounded the government's legislative programme, brought to the fore this constitutional question.

Unionists looked to the house of lords to temper the government's radical programme. The Unionist opposition to the government was not, though, based solely on class antagonism and calculations of electoral advantage: Balfour and Lansdowne (Unionist leaders in the Commons and Lords, respectively) also harked back to the 'referendal' role of the house of lords, and the notion that the Lords could be the 'watchdog of the Constitution', especially in the face of an emasculated house of commons.[3]

Within a year of the election, the Liberal government had run into problems in the house of lords: the Lords had blocked the Education Bill in 1906, and looked likely to cause continuing problems for the government. The king's speech on 12 February 1907 gave notice that reform of the Lords would be considered: 'Serious questions affecting the working of our Parliamentary system have arisen from unfortunate differences between the two Houses. My Ministers have this important subject under consideration with a view to a solution of the difficulty.'[4] The cabinet considered two options to temper the power of the Lords: joint sittings, and a suspensory veto.

2.1.2. Ripon Plan

Following preliminary discussions in February 1907, the cabinet referred the house of lords' question to a cabinet committee under the lord chancellor, Lord Loreburn. The following month, the committee produced a near-unanimous report, which

---

[2] I. Richard and D. Welfare, *Unfinished Business: Reforming the House of Lords* (1998).

[3] J. Ridley, 'The Unionist Opposition and the House of Lords, 1906–1910', *Parliamentary History*, xi (1992), 236. Ironically, perhaps, Balfour had been 'largely responsible' for the tightening of control of government over opposition in the house of commons, under Salisbury's premiership in the late 19th century: Ridley, 'The Unionist Opposition', 235.

[4] Hansard, *Lords Debates*, 4th ser., clxix, col. 1: 12 Feb. 1907.

rejected a number of possibilities, including veto limitation. Reconstruction of the house of lords was turned down, on the grounds that it would strengthen the Lords against the Commons. Referring disputes to a referendum was dismissed, because it would place the importance of the two Houses on an equal footing. Veto limitation was rejected, because the committee thought that this: 'would amount in effect to the abolition of the second chamber and would therefore provoke maximum resistance'. The committee, instead, recommended joint sittings of the house of commons and house of lords as a means of resolving dispute: the proposal was that, after a session's delay, the bill would be placed before a joint sitting of the house of commons (670 members) and 100 peers (of whom up to 20 would be from the government), and the vote of this meeting would determine the fate of the bill. This quickly, though erroneously, became known as the Ripon plan. The committee, though sure of the superiority of its proposals over veto limitation, was unsure whether its proposals would satisfy Liberal Party opinion.[5]

2.1.3. Suspensory Veto

The prime minister thought that joint sittings would satisfy neither Liberal opinion nor the needs of the House. He preferred 'the more drastic method of the one year's veto',[6] although he acknowledged that this might be a minority view, and would be controversial. The idea of the house of lords having a suspensory veto over proposals from the Commons had a long heritage. It had been proposed by the political philosopher, James Mill, in 1836, and popularised in a series of speeches by the politician, John Bright MP, from 1883 onwards.[7] The unpopularity of joint sittings with the party was confirmed on re-examination in June. The personal intervention of Campbell-Bannerman was essential in converting his cabinet to support the suspensory veto; but the price for this was to accept, on the insistence of Lord Crewe (never a convert to the suspensory veto) that a corollary must be an amendment to the Septennial Act to shorten the duration of a parliament from seven years to five.[8]

The suspensory veto proposal, having been agreed by the cabinet, was outlined by Campbell-Bannerman in a speech to the house of commons on 24 June 1907. On 26 June, after a difficult three-day debate, the house of commons, on a motion by the prime minister, resolved by 432 to 147: 'That, in order to give effect to the will of the people as expressed by their elected representatives, it is necessary that the power of the other House to alter or reject Bills passed by this House should be so restricted

---

[5] C.C. Weston, 'The Liberal Leadership and the Lords' Veto, 1907–1910', *Historical Journal*, xi (1968), 510.

[6] Campbell-Bannerman to Lord Knollys, 25 Mar. 1907, quoted in A.S. King, 'Some Aspects of the History of the Liberal Party in Britain', University of Oxford DPhil, 1962, p. 104.

[7] James Mill had written in 1836: 'Let it be enacted that if a bill, which has been passed by the House of Commons, and thrown out by the House of Lords, is renewed in the House of Commons in the next session of Parliament, and passed, but again thrown out by the House of Lords, it shall, if passed a third time in the House, of Commons, be law without being sent again to the Lords': James Mill, 'Aristocracy', *London Review*, (Jan. 1836), quoted in Alfred L.P. Dennis, 'The Parliament Act of 1911 II', *The American Political Science Review*, vi (1912), 393. This passage of Mill was quoted in the debates on the Parliament Bill by Mr Needham: Hansard, *Commons Debates*, 5th ser., xxv, col. 1734: 15 May 1911.

[8] Weston, 'Liberal Leadership', 520.

by Law as to secure that within the limits of a single Parliament the final decision of the Commons shall prevail.'[9] The clear view of the Commons was in favour of veto limitation, despite 20 Liberals and Irish MPs voting for a Labour amendment which had called for abolition.

The veto limitation plan embodied effectiveness against the power of the Lords, and simplicity and clarity of purpose; but the government was unable to effect it straight away. If the bill was rejected by the peers (as it would be, for the government lacked a specific mandate), then it would be impossible for the Liberals to remain in government; but it would, without other cause, be too risky to go to the country on the issue of veto limitation alone. If the powers of the house of lords were to be restricted, then a trigger would have to be found.

2.2. *What Led the Government to Act?*

It is not clear that Lloyd George designed the 1909 budget to be that trigger; indeed, it is probable that Lloyd George hoped to bypass the peers with his budget. But the budget became the clearest and most significant example of the systematic wrecking to which the Unionist majority in the house of lords subjected the government's legislative programme in the 1906–9 parliament.[10] The Finance Bill itself had been set up as a no-win situation for the Conservative peers. When, in mid 1909, Liberal popularity in the country began to rise, Lloyd George began to scent blood.

The cabinet, though, hardly discussed constitutional questions throughout its intense sessions on the implications of budget rejection in October and November 1909, notwithstanding the recirculation of their 1907 memoranda on veto limitation.[11] When the Finance Bill was refused a second reading by the Lords on 30 November, the Commons' reaction was to pass a resolution reasserting that it was the sole authority over financial matters;[12] the Commons did not vote on veto limitation. At the subsequent general election, most Liberal candidates argued for veto limitation, and said nothing of broader reform.

The January 1910 election resulted in what Jenkins terms a 'sufficient majority'; but which Le May prefers to describe as not giving anyone a mandate for anything:[13] the Liberals lost about 100 seats to the Unionists; other parties were largely unchanged. With the Liberal majority obliterated, it was dependent on support from John Redmond's Irish Nationalists, and from the Labour Party. These parties offered an anti-Unionist majority of about 120; but the price for this support was a guarantee to deliver Irish home rule.

---

[9] Hansard, *Commons Debates*, 4th ser., clxxvi, col. 1523: 26 June 1907.

[10] See, e.g., R. Jenkins, *Mr Balfour's Poodle* (1954); N. Blewett, *The Peers, the Parties and the People: The General Elections of 1910* (1972); B.K. Murray, *The People's Budget 1909/10* (Oxford, 1980).

[11] King, 'Some Aspects', 111–12.

[12] 'That the action of the House of Lords . . . is a breach of the Constitution and a usurpation of the rights of the Commons': Hansard, *Commons Debates*, 5th ser., xiii, cols 546–81: 2 Dec. 1909.

[13] Jenkins, *Poodle*, 193. G.H.L. Le May, *The Victorian Constitution: Conventions, Usages and Contingencies* (1979), 196.

2.2.1. Campbell-Bannerman Plan Prevailed

Given the personal importance of Campbell-Bannerman in persuading the cabinet to adopt the suspensory veto plan, it is, perhaps, surprising that the suspensory veto outlived Campbell-Bannerman, who died within a year of the of the 1907 house of commons' resolutions. Asquith, his successor as prime minister, had preferred the Ripon plan. There are three key reasons why the suspensory veto prevailed over wider reform: the pressure for veto limitation from Irish MPs; the preoccupation of Edward Grey, who was the strongest advocate within the cabinet of reform of composition, with foreign affairs; and the lack of inclination on the part of Asquith to innovate.

The Irish leaders Redmond and O'Connor told the cabinet in February 1910 that they could not support the budget until they had seen – and approved – the government's proposals for limiting the house of lords' veto. Earlier that month, the cabinet had reached no definite decision on whether to support veto limitation alone, or reform. But the position of the Irish sealed the fate of reform. The Irish MPs had voted against the budget when the Liberals had a majority in 1909; now that their support was necessary the Irish MPs required a firm assurance that veto limitation, which, in turn, was a prerequisite to secure home rule against opposition from the Lords, was credible. Wider reform would take too long to discuss and agree, and any bill for reform would have uncertain prospects, so the cabinet had little choice if it was to ensure that the budget passed in 1910.

The second factor against reform was Grey's focus on his foreign affairs portfolio. He, consequently, had less time to develop ideas for reform and to persuade his cabinet colleagues to support reform. Moreover, his absence on foreign affairs work meant that he became distanced from rank-and-file Liberal Party members, whose appetite to support reform was limited. Grey's support for reform derived from his genuinely-held belief in two-chamber government and his concern that to concentrate on powers would not solve the underlying causes of the problems. Grey continued to argue strongly within the cabinet for reform over veto limitation.[14]

Asquith may not have abandoned his preference for the Ripon plan over the suspensory veto;[15] but his lack of enthusiasm for any particular proposal for change in the house of lords meant that he was able to steer the debate, but not significantly to influence it. This was, arguably, an optimal position: some senior colleagues strongly supported reform; but if the cabinet backed reform, there was a risk that some ministers would resign and the Irish MPs and some Liberal back benchers would rebel. On 26 February 1910 Asquith steered his cabinet to accept in principle that veto limitation should come first, whilst leaving open the suggestion that more radical legislation on the composition of the upper House could follow. Three veto limitation resolutions were agreed by the cabinet on 11 March.[16]

Two key cabinet meetings determined that powers, and not composition, would form the basis of a bill on the house of lords. On 31 March, the cabinet decided to curtail debate on the veto resolutions and reintroduce the budget in mid-April. If the cabinet could be sure that there would be popular support for overcoming Lords' resistance to

---

[14] King, 'Some Aspects', 136.

[15] Weston, 'Liberal Leadership', 520–2.

[16] A resolution, suggesting that, upon the passage of the other three proposals, the house of lords should be replaced by a directly-elected second chamber, had been drafted for these cabinet discussions but was not put.

a Parliament Bill through swamping with new peerage creations, the government could go to the country and seek the Lords' capitulation on the bill. The decisive cabinet came on 13 April: the cabinet resolved to force the acceptance of the budget on the Irish members by conflating the budget issue with the question of the house of lords' veto.

The cabinet's resolutions had been tabled in the house of commons on 21 March; but, following the cabinet's decision to press forward with the budget during mid-April, discussions on these resolutions began in earnest in committee in the Commons on 11 April 1910, and continued in committee through 12 and 13 April. The cabinet met, also, on each of these days, 'in the unusually pressing exigencies of the existing situation', but failed to reach firm conclusions until 13 April.[17] That decisive cabinet on 13 April determined to curtail debate on the veto resolutions and put them to the vote in the House: should the resolutions be agreed by the Commons, but rejected by the Lords, then the government would seek the necessary steps to give statutory effect to the resolutions in the present parliament; *in extremis* the government would advise a dissolution, though only under the condition that the legislation would prevail after the election.[18] By the end of 14 April, all the resolutions on the Lords' veto had been passed by the house of commons with majorities of between 98 and 106. The resolutions were as follows:[19]

1. That it is expedient that the House of Lords be disabled by Law from rejecting or amending a Money Bill, but that any such limitation by Law shall not be taken to diminish or qualify the existing rights and privileges of the House of Commons.

   For the purpose of this Resolution a Bill shall be considered a Money Bill if, in the opinion of the Speaker, it contains only provisions dealing with all or any of the following subjects, namely, the imposition, repeal, remission, alteration, or regulation of taxation; charges on the Consolidated Fund or the provision of money by Parliament; Supply; the appropriation, control, or regulation of public money; the raising or guarantee of any loan or the repayment thereof; or matters incidental to those subjects or any of them.

2. That it is expedient that the powers of the House of Lords, as respects Bills other than Money Bills, be restricted by Law, so that any such Bill which has passed the House of Commons in three successive Sessions and; having been sent up to the House of Lords at least one month before the end of the Session, has been rejected by that House in each of those Sessions, shall become Law without the consent of the House of Lords on the Royal Assent being declared: Provided that at least two years shall have elapsed between the date of the first introduction of the Bill in the House of Commons and the date on which it passes the House of Commons for the third time.

   For the purposes of this Resolution a Bill shall be treated as rejected by the House of Lords if it has not been passed by the House of Lords either without Amendment or with such Amendments only as may be agreed upon by both Houses.

3. That it is expedient to limit the duration of Parliament to five years.

[17] TNA, CAB 41/40/9: 13 Apr. 1910.
[18] TNA, CAB 41/40/9: 13 Apr. 1910.
[19] Hansard, *Commons Debates*, 5th ser., xvi, cols 1531–47: 14 Apr. 1910.

Immediately following the acceptance of these resolutions, Asquith introduced the Parliament Bill 1910.[20] It was expected that the Parliament Bill 1910 would be further discussed in the Commons later in April.[21]

On 27 April, the Commons gave the Finance Bill its third reading. The following day, the Lords accepted the mandate of the January 1910 election and passed the Finance Bill without a vote.[22] It was felt that the period of uncertainty was now over, and the budget having been passed, 'the Cabinet began to prepare for a midsummer election', resolved that it must secure, before the election was called, a guarantee that the king would, if necessary, create peers to secure the passage of either the budget or the Parliament Bill.[23]

2.2.2. Constitutional Conference

The planned midsummer 1910 election did not, however, take place. The unexpected death of King Edward VII on 6 May 1910 delayed proceedings. The government's policy was now that a general election could not take place before they had secured guarantees that, should the house of lords oppose veto limitation after the election, the king would be prepared to create sufficient peers to overcome this opposition. King Edward VII had been informed of this before his death; but it was felt that, following the accession of George V, 'for the monarch to assume such a course of action so early in his reign was only inviting miscalculation and criticism',[24] and that it was, therefore, unduly early in his reign to extract such assurances from the new king.

This delay might have provided a window of opportunity for alternative plans to veto limitation to be reopened. Several members of the Liberal government, including Grey, Crewe, and possibly Asquith himself, began once more to pursue the Ripon plan.[25] An alternative approach, which held more sway, was that the constitutional hiatus following the death of the king might provide an opportunity for compromise between government and opposition on the question of the powers of the Lords. Some Liberal proponents of veto limitation were reluctant to enter negotiations, lest the cabinet's position become discredited in the eyes of the wider Liberal Party and amongst the Irish MPs; but they yielded to the feeling that 'public opinion was overwhelmingly in favour of interparty negotiations'.[26]

The constitutional conference met 22 times between 17 June and 10 November, and received full details of recent proposals for settling the house of lords' question.[27] The

[20] Hansard, *Commons Debates*, 5th ser., xvi, col. 1547: 14 Apr. 1910.

[21] Asquith said, in an answer to an oral question on 21 April: 'I hope sometime next week': Hansard, *Commons Debates*, 5th ser., xvi, col. 2303: 21 Apr. 1910.

[22] V. Bogdanor, *Monarchy and the Constitution* (Oxford, 1995), 114.

[23] Blewett, *Peers*, 153.

[24] J.D. Fair, *British Interparty Conferences: A Study of the Procedure of Conciliation in British Politics, 1867–1921* (Oxford, 1980), 83.

[25] Weston, 'Liberal Leadership', 522–4.

[26] Fair, *Interparty Conferences*, 83.

[27] TNA, CAB 37/103/24: 22 June 1910.

question of the Lords' powers over financial legislation, which had been at the heart of the dispute over the budget and the subsequent need to consider veto limitation, proved uncontroversial. More problematic were the Conservatives' arguments that legislation affecting constitutional matters, including home rule, should be subject to legislative safeguards – a position which was incompatible with the Liberals' desire to hold the power to pursue radical measures, and their immediate need to guarantee home rule. The Ripon plan was resurgent, and Asquith seemed willing to consider joint sittings of the two houses of parliament as a means of resolving disputes, as an alternative to the suspensory veto; but no agreement could be found on the size of the delegation that the house of lords would send to a joint sitting.[28] In any case, the Unionists preferred referral to a referendum to either joint sittings or right of the upper House to force a general election as a way of settling constitutional questions. And any suggestion that Asquith might consider compromising with the Conservatives was soon offset by Lloyd George's absolute refusal seriously to consider thoroughgoing second chamber reform.[29] The key problem impeding progress at the constitutional conference was not the issues of powers and composition themselves, but rather the effect of any possible solution on the imminent question of Irish home rule. Whilst 'during the course of their twenty-two sittings the members of this colloquy wrestled with every form of constitutional change which confronted the nation', concluded John D. Fair, the only tangible effect of the constitutional conference 'was to delay a settlement of the House of Lords question for six months after the death of King Edward'.[30]

As soon as the conference was disbanded, the cabinet determined to dissolve parliament and to fight a general election on the twin questions of the budget and the veto limitation. With some difficulty, Asquith secured the promise for peerage creations from King George V that he had from the king's father several months earlier, advising the monarch on 15 November 1910 that he would not advise a dissolution unless the king promised, if necessary, to create peers to ensure the government's policy. Asquith did so by assuring the king that if the policy was publicised, he felt it necessary to keep 'the name of the King out of the sphere of party & electoral controversy'.[31] The assurance came from the king the following day.

The house of lords' question dominated the campaign for the December 1910 general election and for the first time peers broke prevailing convention (or practice) by campaigning alongside house of commons' candidates. The election left the composition of the house of commons almost unchanged: Liberals 272 (down three), Conservatives 272 (down one), Labour 42 (up two), Irish Party 84 (up two). The Liberal government remained dependent on the support of the Irish and Labour MPs. The government, therefore, had an electoral mandate to pursue its stated election policy of limiting the Lords' veto.

[28] Weston, 'Liberal Leadership', 523–33.

[29] Fair, *Interparty Conferences*, 86–91.

[30] Fair, *Interparty Conferences*, 102.

[31] TNA, CAB 41/38/1: 15 Nov. 1910.

3. *What Happened to the Bill in its Passage through Parliament?*

3.1. *Passage through Parliament*

The Parliament Bill that Asquith introduced to the Commons on 21 February 1911[32] was identical to the bill that had been given a first reading in the Commons ten months earlier, the purpose of which was 'to make provision with respect to the powers of the House of Lords in relation to those of the House of Commons, and to limit the duration of Parliament'.[33] 'Since then', said the prime minister, introducing the 1911 bill, 'that Bill has been submitted definitely and specifically to the electorate of the country, with the result that they have returned to this House a majority in its favour in the United Kingdom of, I suppose, something like 120, and in Great Britain of not less than sixty.'[34]

The Parliament Bill of 1911 was intended 'to make provision with respect to the powers of the House of Lords in relation to those of the House of Commons, and to limit the duration of Parliament'.[35] The bill sought to take away the Lords' powers to amend or to delay certified money bills, to replace the Lords' veto over other primary legislation which emanated from the Commons with a delay of approximately two years, and to shorten the maximum duration of a parliament from seven to five years. The Lords' powers over secondary legislation, and over primary legislation originating in the house of lords, remained unaffected. The principle behind the Parliament Bill of 1911 was, therefore, to allow a government, with a majority in the house of commons, to give effect to its legislative programme.

3.2. *Did it Arouse Opposition in Either or Both Houses?*

The committee stage of the bill in the Commons lasted 13 days, during which numerous amendments were moved, though none was successful. Several of these were moved again at the report stage; but, again, they did not prevail. The bill passed all its Commons' stages without incident and left the house of commons, having received its third reading on 15 May 1911.

The Lords gave the bill an unopposed second reading on 29 May after a four-day debate, and then proceeded to amend the bill heavily in the committee of the whole House in late June and early July, in particular so as to make provision to ensure a referendum on bills of constitutional importance. The Lords' opposition to the bill was fundamental, and there was a substantial risk that the Lords would seek to defeat the bill as a whole.

Against the backdrop of Lords' opposition, Asquith wrote to Balfour and Lansdowne on 20 July 1911, stating the assurances he had received from the king about peerage creation. The letter from Asquith transformed the position of the Unionist leadership. Balfour knew that he did not have sufficient support in the house of commons to form

---

[32] Hansard, *Commons Debates*, 5th ser., xxi, cols 1742–851: 21 Feb. 1911.

[33] Hansard, *Commons Debates*, 5th ser., xvi, col. 1547: 14 Apr. 1910.

[34] Hansard, *Commons Debates*, 5th ser., xxi, col. 1742: 21 Feb. 1911 (Asquith).

[35] Hansard, *Commons Debates*, 5th ser., xxi, col. 1742: 21 Feb. 1911 (Asquith).

a government, and a third general election in quick succession, this time on the Parliament Bill of 1911, was out of the question. Balfour, therefore, realized that the king would have little choice but to accede to a request from Asquith for the creation of peers.[36] Balfour turned against the 'ditchers' (or die-hards), who had been resolved to 'die in the last ditch' and oppose the Parliament Bill without regard to the consequences, though he could not bring himself to side with the 'hedgers' (those Unionists who supported the bill), who he saw as surrendering their Unionist principles to the government.[37] Lansdowne, fearing swamping of the Lords, advocated surrender over the Parliament Bill, and in an uncharacteristic reversal of their relationship, Lansdowne succeeded in imposing this view on a reluctant Balfour. The Unionist leadership, therefore, recommended following Wellington's precedent from 1832: advocating abstention when the bill returned to the Lords; but stopping short of voting for the bill.[38] Lansdowne publicly encouraged Unionist peers to abstain when the bill returned to the Lords.

Persuading the 'ditchers' away from their determined course was, however, difficult. Even with some Unionist peers abstaining, the 'ditchers' were numerous enough to vote down the bill. Lansdowne's argument for surrender drove some die-hard peers into open revolt. Discussions ensued behind the scenes, encouraged by Lord Newton, to ensure that sufficient Unionist peers would vote in favour of the bill to allow it to be carried against the continuing resistance from the die-hards. After two further days of debate, the Lords withdrew its insistence on amendments in the face of Commons' opposition, and the Parliament Bill passed the Lords on 11 August by 131 to 114: 83 Liberals, 13 bishops, and 35 Unionists (the so-called 'Judas peers')[39] voted in favour, with Unionists and some backwoodsmen against. The royal assent was given, with the consent of both Houses, on 18 August 1911.

3.3. Did Either or Both Houses Affect the Content?

Despite the lengthy debates in the two Houses, the Parliament Bill remained only lightly amended during its passage through parliament. Only four principal amendments to the bill were enacted. Perhaps the most significant of these amendments was to section 2 of the bill, which was altered in the house of lords to ensure that peers retained an absolute veto over provisional order confirmation bills[40] and any 'Bill containing any provision to extend the duration of Parliament beyond five years'. The provision protecting bills to extend the duration of parliament had been moved by Earl Winterton (an MP) and

[36] J. Ridley, 'Leadership and Management in the Conservative Party in Parliament, 1906–1914', University of Oxford DPhil, 1985, p. 141.

[37] On the die-hards, and the fact that they were not primarily backwoodsmen, see G.D. Phillips, *The Diehards: Aristocratic Society and Politics in Edwardian England* (Harvard, 1979).

[38] D. Southern, 'Lord Newton, the Conservative Peers and the Parliament Act of 1911', *English Historical Review*, xcvi (1981), 836.

[39] On the Judas peers, see Southern, 'Lord Newton'; C.C. Weston and P. Kelvin, 'The "Judas Group" and the Parliament Bill of 1911', *English Historical Review*, xcix (1984), 551–63.

[40] No such bills have been introduced since 1980, and the standing orders now consider this procedure to have fallen into disuse.

others in the debates on the Commons' resolutions in 1910[41] and had, at that time, been opposed by the government, and defeated. But it was accepted by the Commons on consideration of Lords' amendments, and appeared in the act. The Commons accepted a government amendment which required that before giving his certificate: 'that it is a Money Bill', 'the Speaker shall consult, if practicable, two members to be appointed'. A further amendment, accepted by the Commons, answered opposition concerns that the bill should not interfere with local taxation: clause 1(2) of the bill was amended to read: 'In this subsection the expressions "taxation", "public money", and "loan" respectively do not include any taxation, money, or loan raised by local authorities or bodies for local purposes.' The fourth substantive amendment was to delete clause 1(4), which had originally read: 'No amendment shall be allowed to a Money Bill which, in the opinion of the Speaker of the House of Commons, is such as to prevent the Bill retaining the character of a Money Bill': the government determined that it would be unduly restrictive of parliamentary procedure. Other amendments were defeated, or not put.[42]

4. What were the Consequences of the Measure?

The most important short-term consequence of the Parliament Act 1911 was the passage of the Finance Bill the previous year. Without cast-iron guarantees to ensure that the Parliament Bill 1910 eventually became law, the crucial support of the Irish MPs for the budget, of which they had not initially been in favour, would have been lost. The Irish MPs were insistent upon the Parliament Act because it was necessary to overcome peers' resistance to Irish home rule; realization of home rule, through the passage of the Government of Ireland Act in 1914, was, therefore, a second short-term consequence of the Parliament Act 1911. The act had its immediate planned effect of ensuring the government's budget, and eradicating the absolute formal legislative veto of the Lords over the government's programme.

However, the Parliament Act left the house of lords with a formidable range of powers, and, arguably, it had as much exercisable power as it had before the 1909 budget crisis. In restricting the power of the Lords to veto most bills, the Parliament Act had also, conversely, accepted that the upper House could delay government bills for up to two years. Because the political imbalance in the composition of the house of lords remained untouched by the Parliament Act, this delaying power, combined with the shortening of the duration of a parliament to five years, in effect, conferred a 'referendal power' on the Lords – the power to refer issues to the people at the next election – over any measure introduced after the third session of a parliament. Moreover, the act took away the routine excuse for Asquith resisting the demands of nonconformists and nationalists – that the Lords would block the legislation.[43] The act was not, therefore, a panacea for the legislative difficulties of a progressive government.

---

[41] Hansard, *Commons Debates*, 5th ser., xvi, col. 1252: 13 Apr. 1910.

[42] On the amendments to the bill, see Jaconelli, 'Parliament Bill', 277–96.

[43] A. Adonis, *Making Aristocracy Work* (Oxford, 1993), 158.

4.1. *Constitutional Implications and Legacy*

The Parliament Act 1911, in ending the equal legislative power of the two houses of parliament, resolved long-standing disagreements over the proper constitutional balance between peers and the elected house of commons by allowing a procedure by which the cabinet-controlled house of commons could prevail over the hereditary-dominated house of lords. The act 'obliged the Unionist leadership to re-evaluate the role of the Lords in Tory/Unionist politics, much as Salisbury had in the late 1860's'.[44] The act's principle, that the upper House should not be able to make and unmake governments, and its principal provision, that the upper House should possess only a suspensory veto over Commons' bills, were both accepted by successive attempts to reform the house of lords across the following 100 years. This inertia may have been because the position reached under the Parliament Act was *an* equilibrium rather than *the optimal* equilibrium, with powers being too substantial for progressive politicians, but too weak for conservatives.

The act also effected a substantial shift in the responsibility for proposing house of lords' reform onto the shoulders of the government. Hitherto, the schemes presented in the 19th or early 20th centuries had been formulated independently of the government, or in opposition to it. From 1909 onwards, successive governments felt it their duty to assume responsibility for formulating plans for house of lords' reform, and no scheme had a significant prospect of being implemented if it did not have support from the government of the day.[45]

The Parliament Act significantly affected the constitutional future of the United Kingdom, not only by establishing the suspensory veto as the starting point for future proposals relating to powers; but also because it enabled constitutional reform (including to the Lords' powers) to be passed without the agreement of the upper House. Indeed, all of the seven acts passed under the Parliament Act procedures[46] can be said to be constitutional in nature, either because they change aspects of the formal constitution, or because they affect significant aspects of human rights. Such actions were very much in the minds of those who supported the Parliament Act; indeed, an amendment to restrict its application to constitutional legislation was explicitly rejected.

One of these constitutional reforms made possible by the Parliament Act 1911 was the further limitation of the period of the Lords' suspensory veto by the Parliament Act 1949. The validity of the Parliament Act 1949, and, therefore, of legislation passed under its provisions, was subsequently doubted by some constitutional lawyers.[47] These

---

[44] Adonis, *Making Aristocracy Work*, 157.

[45] E.g., Lord Curzon wrote, in 1921: 'practically for the first time the Government itself would be called upon to produce a scheme of Reform for which it must assume full responsibility': Parliamentary Archives, PO/300/11: HLC 1st Conclusions, 26 Oct. 1921.

[46] The Welsh Church Act 1914 (which disestablished the Church in Wales), the Government of Ireland Act 1914 (which established home rule for Ireland), the Parliament Act 1949 (which further limited the Lords' suspensory veto over Commons' bills), the War Crimes Act 1991 (which retrospectively authorised the prosecution of alleged war criminals from the Second World War), the European Parliamentary Elections Act 1999 (which provided for a closed-list proportional voting system for these elections), the Sexual Offences (Amendment) Act 2000 (which, *inter alia*, responded to a European Convention on Human Rights (ECHR) ruling to equalise the age of consent for homosexual and heterosexual activity), and the Hunting Act 2004 (which banned the hunting of wild animals with dogs).

[47] See H.W.R. Wade, 'The Basis of Legal Sovereignty', *Cambridge Law Journal*, xiii (1955), 172–97.

authorities argued that the Parliament Act 1911 had created a delegated authority, in the king and the house of commons, to legislate in certain circumstances without the consent of the house of lords, and since this was a delegated authority it could not further be amended without the consent of the house of lords. The applicability of the procedure under the Parliament Act 1911 to its own amendment was not, however, raised by the cabinet's advisors during its consideration in 1945–9 of proposals that eventually became the Parliament Act 1949.

The appellate committee of the house of lords considered in *Jackson* the argument that the Parliament Act 1949 was invalid and unanimously rejected it.[48] The power to legislate without the consent of the Lords, conferred under the Parliament Act 1911, was restricted only by the explicit exceptions contained in that act, and not by any implied constraints. Laws passed under the Parliament Act 1911 had the character of primary legislation, not delegated legislation. The law lords concluded that the enactment of the Parliament Act 1949 was a valid application of the powers conferred under the Parliament Act 1911, and, therefore, that subsequent legislation passed under these acts was likewise valid.[49] The ability to use the Parliament Act 1911 to reduce the period of the Lords' suspensory veto was, perhaps, unforeseen (indeed, unconsidered) by Asquith's government in 1909–11; but it was not unintended.

4.1.1. Other Powers

Notwithstanding its removal of the Lords' veto over Commons' bills, the Parliament Act left the house of lords with substantial powers over other areas of legislation. The Lords retains a veto over any bill which begins its legislative passage in the house of lords, a power that can significantly affect how government legislation is planned. The house of lords also retains a veto over subordinate legislation. This was not a significant consideration in 1911, and was not considered in 1947–9, when the Parliament Act was amended. However, the power has been used three times – in 1968 (to reject the Southern Rhodesia (United Nations Sanctions) Order), and in 2000 (when two provisions relating to the Greater London Authority were rejected) – even though these measures were all subsequently passed by the house of lords without undue delay. The veto power over secondary legislation is often now considered unusable because of its severity.

4.1.2. Reform of Composition

The Parliament Act shaped the future course of the reform of the composition of the house of lords; but it did not lead to the subsequent creation of 'a Second Chamber

---

[48] Though for varying reasons: see *Jackson and others (Appellants) v. Her Majesty's Attorney General (Respondent)*, [2005] UKHL 56.

[49] Note, however, that a majority of the law lords rejected the notion that the Parliament Act could be amended under its own powers to allow an extension to the duration of a parliament, first through the removal of the restriction on extending a parliament, and then by extending the parliament. Lord Bingham of Cornhill, in a minority view, thought that a two-stage approach would work; see also Jaconelli, 'Parliament Bill', 296 n. 64.

constituted on a popular instead of a hereditary basis', to which the preamble of the act aspired. It is true that some within the cabinet – most notably Grey, upon whose insistence the preamble had been inserted into the bill – hoped that the curtailment of the Lords' veto would lead to a more thoroughgoing reform of the upper House. But the support for the 'Campbell-Bannerman plan' of the suspensory veto had become widespread amongst the Liberal rank and file. Any reform to composition would have augmented the power of the upper House, and thereby its ability to impede the enactment of the social welfare policies to which the Liberals had become committed. Asquith's cabinet returned briefly to the question of further reform in the second half of 1912,[50] but the cabinet never came to a binding conclusion on composition. Although Lords' reform was mentioned in the king's speech of 1913, the Asquith cabinet never discussed the matter after that year. The onset of war in November 1914 pushed Lords' reform off the political agenda. As far as much of the Liberal Party had been concerned at the time, the Parliament Act was not 'unfinished business'.

The preamble to the Parliament Act affected the tenor of debate on Lords' reform in subsequent years. Although the preamble had no legal force, and its sentiment had no wide base of support within the Liberal Party, Balfour and his Conservative colleagues still used it as the basis for arguments that Britain existed under an 'interim constitution'.[51] But the reform of composition was a second-order question for successive governments, which saw that any substantial reform to composition, in addition to being difficult to agree and time-consuming to legislate for, would inevitably create an emboldened upper House, which would, therefore, be more likely to use the substantial powers which remained to it, notwithstanding, or perhaps because of, the Parliament Act.

5. *Conclusion*

At the heart of the Parliament Act were two paradoxes. First, through restriction of the Lords' powers the Commons was at risk of legitimating a more moderate suspensory veto which could, at least in theory, make the Lords more powerful in peacetime. Second, the restriction of powers was so strong that there was no longer a desire to increase power by changing composition. The Parliament Bill, therefore, both raised the curtain on a century of constitutional reform, made easier to enact by its provisions, and simultaneously made house of lords' reform more difficult to achieve for the next 100 years.

---

[50] TNA, CAB 41/33/62: 7 Aug. 1912; CAB 37/113/134: 17 Dec. 1912 (note by Herbert Samuel).
[51] Balfour memorandum of 1913, quoted in Bogdanor, *Monarchy*, 123.

Laying the Foundations of the Modern Voting System: The Representation of the People Act 1918

ROBERT BLACKBURN

This article studies the preparation, passage, and consequences of the Representation of the People Act 1918. Commonly known as the fourth and last of the 'Reform Acts' starting in 1832, that transformed the politics of Great Britain into a parliamentary democracy, this major piece of constitutional legislation laid the foundations for the country's present-day voting and electoral system. Most famous for introducing universal adult suffrage and the women's vote, it initiated a large number of new concepts and practices in elections, including making residency in a constituency the basis of the right to vote, whilst institutionalising the first-past-the-post method of election instead of proportional representation (PR). As a political and constitutional process for reform, it was virtually unique in dealing with a range of principles and issues that were deeply controversial, yet ones that were debated and enacted in a spirit of concord amongst parliamentarians about the overriding need for civil reconstruction in the post-war era.

Keywords: alternative vote (AV); ballot; electoral register; franchise; house of commons; house of lords; legislation; proportional representation (PR); Reform Acts; Representation of the People Bill; suffragettes

The Representation of the People Act 1918 established the universal franchise and ushered in a wide range of fundamental elements of the modern voting and electoral system. It answered questions of reform that had been the subject of heated political debate throughout the previous half-century, ranging from votes for women to proportional representation (PR). Not just the huge importance of its content, but also the manner of its presentation and passage, make it one of the greatest achievements of constitutional reform in the 20th century. Unlike almost all other reforms of a seismic nature in British history, the Representation of the People Bill, though deeply controversial in its provisions, was enacted in a spirit of relative co-operation, with politicians on all sides willing to accept the need to reach agreement.

The bill was presented for its first reading in the house of commons on 15 May 1917 and received its royal assent on 6 February 1918. What is most immediately striking about the timing and passage of this particular piece of constitutional legislation is the hugely time-consuming and complex preparations for the legislation (set out in 47 sections and nine schedules, repealing 50 statutes and modifying 57 others), and the very lengthy parliamentary debates and discussions on the bill, all taking place during the most traumatic and devastating war Britain had ever faced. Yet this concurrence of electoral reform and war was in large measure the key to the bill's success. For the years of war in 1914–18, when vast numbers of troops were killed and injured, leaving hardly a family in the country untouched by tragedy, generated a common spirit across the political spectrum that the post-war state of the country must be a better place ('a land fit for heroes') for all. A prevalent view at Westminster was that seemingly intractable domestic problems, particularly those relating to citizenship, ought to be confronted and resolved towards that end.

1. *The Changes Made by the Act*

Section 1 of the bill, as enacted, declared that a man shall be entitled to be registered as a parliamentary elector for a constituency if he is of full age and not subject to any legal incapacity and has the requisite residence qualification. Residency in a constituency, therefore, became the basis for the franchise, which has remained the case in election law ever since. A qualifying period of residence was made necessary by the act, put at six months (reduced by later legislation[1] and subsequently replaced by a fixed date in the year and today superseded by a rolling electoral register[2]). Section 5 of the act made special provisions for persons serving on war service, allowing them to be registered to vote in any constituency where they could have been registered if not for their war service.

Section 4 of the act granted the franchise to women, but at a higher age than men, 30 years. Oddly, later the same year parliament enacted the Parliament (Qualification of Women) Act 1918, which removed the disqualification from membership of the house of commons of persons on the basis of their gender or marital status. So for some years after the 1918 act, a women might be an MP and able to vote on national legislation, but ineligible to cast a vote at a general election. The pressure towards equal franchise rights led to the Representation of the People Act 1928, reducing the age of the female franchise to 21 years, in line with men.

The practice of plural voting was abolished, the act providing that a person who owned several houses and was, therefore, registered in several constituencies could only vote in one of the constituencies (of their choice).[3] The business premises franchise remained, allowing owners of business premises an additional vote in the constituency where the premises were.[4] So, too, there remained the university franchise, allowing graduates of certain universities, each clustered as a notional constituency, an additional vote.[5] However, the act provided that no one could have more than two votes,[6] if they were registered as a residential voter, a business premises owner voter, and a university constituency voter. Important matters of electoral administration were dealt with by the

---

[1] Three months was substituted by the Representation of the People (Economy Provisions) Act 1926, section 9, schedule 3.

[2] See Robert Blackburn, *The Electoral System in Britain* (Basingstoke, 1995), ch. 3; Electoral Administration Act 2006; and Political Parties and Elections Act 2009.

[3] Section 8.

[4] Section 1(b).

[5] Section 2.

[6] Section 8. Section 22 also provided penalties for persons voting more than they were entitled. The business and university franchises were eventually abolished by the Representation of the People Act 1949.

act, including a limited scheme of postal and proxy voting for absent voters,[7] and the requirement that at a general election all constituency polls should take place on the same date. A detailed code of rules and procedures was included for the registration of electors.[8] A financial deposit was required before a person could stand as a parliamentary candidate.[9]

Three independent Boundary Commissions (for England and Wales, Scotland, and Ireland) were set up at the same time as the Representation of the People Bill was introduced into parliament in 1917,[10] leading to their recommendations on a wide-ranging redistribution of seats being incorporated into the body of the legislation.[11] Related to this was the most controversial and disruptive aspect of the bill during its passage through parliament, which was the bill's proposal for adoption of the alternative vote (AV) in single-member constituencies and PR in seats returning more than two members. In the final event, as discussed below, both of these different systems for choosing members in the house of commons were defeated, leaving the simple plurality (first-past-the-post) system to endure throughout the 20th century.

2. *The Historical Background*

The argument for extending the male suffrage, and behind it the case for democracy itself, had been accepted across the political parties by the time the bill was prepared. This transformation in conceptions about political representation had evolved in less than 90 years. Indeed, only 50 years prior to the 1918 act, Walter Bagehot – whose classic work, *The English Constitution*, remains in print – had vehemently opposed any extension of the franchise, referring to the 'bovine stupidity' of the working classes whom he described as 'crowds of people scarcely more civilised than the majority of 2,000 years ago'. Of its negative consequences for the political system, he said:[12]

> The principle of popular government is that the supreme power, the determining efficacy in matters political, resides in the people – not necessarily in the whole people . . . In plain English, what I fear is that both our political parties will bid for the support of the working man; that both of them will promise to do as he likes if he will only tell them what it is; that, as he now holds the casting vote in our affairs, both parties will beg and pray him to give that vote to them. I can conceive of nothing more corrupting or worse for a set of poor ignorant people than that two combinations of well-taught and rich men should constantly offer to defer to their decision, and compete for the office of executing it. *Vox populi* will be *vox diaboli* if it is worked in that manner.

[7] Section 23.
[8] Sections 11–19 and schedule 1.
[9] Sections 26, 27.
[10] Cd. 8576 (14 May 1917); Cd. 8585 (16 May 1917); Cd. 8786 (26 Oct. 1917) respectively.
[11] Section 37 and schedule 9.
[12] *The English Constitution* (1867; Fontana edn 1963), 62, 78, 277.

The 1918 act was known as the fourth 'Reform Act', its predecessors being the Representation of the People Acts passed in 1832, 1867 and 1884.[13] The aim and process of the first of these, the Great Reform Act 1832, was markedly different from that one enacted in 1918.[14] The 1832 act was not driven by democratic ideals – indeed, the architects of the bill 'had not the least intention of introducing democracy'[15] – and the changes made by that statute related essentially to the redistribution of constituencies rather than extending the franchise to ordinary men and women. It did away with the old 'rotten boroughs', notoriously where members were returned to the house of commons from locations where virtually no one resided. It did not increase the size of the national electorate substantially: this changed from 509,391 voters to 720,784 out of a total adult population of over ten million. The triumph of the Great Reform Act was to herald an era of change in a system of political representation that had barely altered since the Glorious Revolution settled the foundations of the constitution in 1688. The real significance of 1832 was not so much what it achieved in itself, as the precedent it set for constitutional change and future reform of a representative process that had remained stagnant over the centuries.[16]

The subject of parliamentary reform and electoral law riveted politicians and lawyers alike throughout the Victorian era, and was the most hotly debated of all constitutional issues. Bills were repeatedly introduced into parliament on some aspect of election law, and intellectuals busied themselves with new schemes of representation.

The next step in extending popular government came with the Representation of the People Act 1867 (the second Reform Act), which doubled the size of the, then, existing electorate from 1,130,372 to 2,231,030 adults, and all but established the principle of 'one household, one vote' in constituency boroughs, though not yet in the counties where a property qualification continued to apply.[17] That glaring discrepancy between town and country became increasingly untenable, and in 1884 another Representation of the People Act (the third Reform Act) was enacted, more than doubling the size of the county electorate. There was now a uniform householder and lodger franchise, in effect giving a vote to every man aged over 21 years who had a decent settled home. As a result of the 1884 act, the size of the electorate became 4,965,618 out of a total adult population of 17,394,014, representing 28.5% of the whole.[18]

In any election to a representative body, the nature of the constituencies adopted is as important to the political outcome as the method of voting. In terms of the future

---

[13] Among the many histories of the electoral system, see I. Machin, *The Rise of Democracy in Britain, 1830–1918* (Basingstoke, 2001); Sir Ivor Jennings, *Party Politics: Vol. 1: Appeal to the People* (Cambridge, 1960); for the period from the Stuarts to Queen Victoria, J. Grego, *A History of Parliamentary Elections* (1892); and for the 20th century, D. Butler, *The Electoral System in Britain since 1918* (2nd edn, Oxford, 1962) and John Curtice, 'The Electoral System', in *The British Constitution in the Twentieth Century*, ed. V. Bogdanor (Oxford, 2003).

[14] In comparison to the parliamentary passage of the 1918 act, the Great Reform Act was deeply acrimonious: see M. Brock, *The Great Reform Act* (1973); E.J. Evans, *The Great Reform Act of 1832* (1983).

[15] A.L. Lowell, *The Government of England* (New York, 1920), 206; and see G. Lowes Dickinson, *The Development of Parliament During the Nineteenth Century* (1895).

[16] Blackburn, *The Electoral System in Britain*, 67.

[17] Though the owners' and long leaseholders' property qualification was reduced from £10 to £5.

[18] S. Gordon, *Our Parliament* (6th edn, 1964), 50–1.

structure of representative government, therefore, an event of very great importance was the constituency review that took place in 1884–5. The Redistribution of Seats Act 1885 radically redrew parliamentary constituency boundaries, and was founded on the principle of broadly similar electoral sizes, having utilised the mechanism of an independent Boundary Commission to carry out the research and prepare recommendations on the redistribution.[19] The outcome of this act was to render single-member constituencies the norm rather than the exception, as had been the case previously, which had major implications for the implementation of PR when it came to be considered in 1917–18.

The state of the law on the ordinary franchise immediately prior to the 1918 act was complicated and difficult to administer.[20] There were at least six different forms of residential qualification to be an elector (and be registered), including: (a) as a householder, provided he had lived in the same parliamentary division for 12 months, and if occupying part of a house that did not have the landlord resident on the same premises; (b) as a freeholder, provided he had owned the property for six months producing 40 shillings income per annum clear of all expenses; (c) as a leaseholder, provided the lease was worth £50 per annum and was for a term not less than 20 years, or the lease was worth at least £5 per annum and was originally created for a term of not less than 60 years; (d) as an occupier, provided the land or tenement was a yearly value of £10 or more; (d) as a lodger, provided he had occupied rooms in the same house for 12 months, and the value of the occupation was £10 or four shillings a week for unfurnished or six shillings a week for furnished rooms; and (e) as a service franchise, where employees including schoolmasters, caretakers, bank managers, servants, and others occupying rooms or houses rent free on their employers' property may exercise a vote so long as their employer is not also resident on the property.

In addition to the complexity of these franchises, there were numerous situations of injustice affecting individuals. The groups of persons who found themselves excluded from the franchise included domestic servants, persons living with their parents and not having their own home, and persons whose work caused them to move homes regularly. In 1902, a schoolteacher wrote a much-talked-about letter to *The Times*, detailing how he was professionally qualified, 40 years old and married, and in receipt of a reasonable income, but because he was much in demand in his work and had regularly moved to better employment, he had never been allowed to vote at a general election.[21] Much more prominently in the public eye, however, due to the public demonstrations and activist work of the suffragettes was the issue of the female vote.[22]

---

[19] It is worth drawing attention to the important statutes enacted during the Victorian era that dealt with electoral matters not requiring attention by the 1918 act and which had dramatically cleaned up the rampant corruption that had existed earlier, notably the Ballot Act 1872 pioneering the secret ballot, and the Corrupt and Illegal Practices Acts 1854 and 1883 outlawing a number of unacceptable electioneering practices.

[20] There was also a separate business premises franchise and a university franchise, both of which were retained by the Representation of the People Act 1918: see above, p. 34.

[21] *The Times*, 30 Aug. 1902.

[22] See below, pp. 43–4; and generally N. Smith, *The British Women's Suffrage Campaign 1866–1928* (1998); P. Bartley, *Votes for Women 1860–1928* (1998); Christabel Pankhurst, *Unshackled: The Story of How We Won the Vote*, ed. Lord Pethick-Lawrence (1959).

3. The Catalyst for the 1918 Act

As so often the case in Britain, the catalyst for this major constitutional reform was an urgent political event. This was the protracted war with Germany and the need to provide a special electoral register suitable for wartime conditions, with mass population movement and hundreds of thousands of soldiers and sailors absent overseas.

A general election was considerably overdue, the previous one having been in December 1910, and one should have taken place towards the end of 1915. It was to have been the first held under the new statutory maximum duration period of five years laid down in section 7 of the Parliament Act 1911,[23] amending the earlier seven years in the Septennial Act 1716. However, a succession of temporary statutory expedients prolonged the life of parliament, in each case for periods of less than one year.[24] Thus section 1(1) of the Parliament and Registration Act 1916 provided that: 'Section seven of the Parliament Act, 1911, shall, in its application to the present Parliament have effect as if five years and eight months were substituted for five years.' Next, section 1 of the Parliament and Local Elections Act 1916 provided: 'Subsection (l) of section one of the Parliament and Registration Act, 1916, shall have effect as if six years and three months were substituted therein for five years and eight months.' Then section 1 of the Parliament and Local Elections Act 1917 laid down that: 'Subsection (l) of section one of the Parliament and Registration Act, 1916, shall have effect as if six years and ten months were substituted therein for five years and eight months; and section one of the Parliament and Local Elections Act, 1916, is hereby repealed.' Finally, section 1 of the Parliament and Local Elections (No. 2) Act 1917 provided: 'Subsection (l) of section one of the Parliament and Registration Act, 1916, shall have effect as if seven years and six months were substituted therein for five years and eight months; and section one of the Parliament and Local Elections Act, 1917, is hereby repealed.' A general election could not be postponed indefinitely, and many parliamentarians did not accept that the war was a sufficient reason for cancelling one in the first place. Lord Parmoor called prolongation 'a constitutional monstrosity',[25] and Bonar Law remarked: 'It is a very invidious thing for any body to prolong its own life.'[26] It was pointed out in the parliamentary debates on the prolongation statutes that elections were not suspended during the Napoleonic wars, the previous great threat to the nation, and in 1914–18 mainland Britain was not part of the theatre of war, save for the occasional Zeppelin bombing raid. The overriding practical reason for not holding an election was the problem of compiling an electoral register for constituencies, which required legislation.

The home secretary, Sir George Cave, therefore brought forward a Special Register Bill in summer 1916. However, this was presented in a half-hearted manner, to say the

---

[23] See Blackburn, *The Electoral System in Britain*, ch. 2.

[24] See Robert Blackburn, *The Meeting of Parliament* (Aldershot, 1990), ch. 3.

[25] Hansard, *Lords Debates*, 5th ser., xx, col. 830: 6 Jan. 1916.

[26] Hansard, *Commons Debates*, 5th ser., cviii, col. 67: 8 July 1918.

least, and was met with strong criticism in parliament.[27] This was due to the issue of a special register opening up a whole raft of other voting reform questions which the bill did not address, and which had been the subject of heated debates throughout the pre-war period of Liberal administrations in 1905–14. In other words, the government's bill to address registration alone stirred up controversies that had lain dormant during the distraction of the war effort, and opened a can of ideological and practical worms that could be dealt with properly only through a comprehensive electoral reform bill.

The solution, the president of the Local Government Board, Walter Long, suggested to the House, was an all-party conference to settle differences of opinion and bring forward an agreed set of proposals for a comprehensive piece of legislation. Advocating this idea to the house of commons, he said:[28]

> I myself believe that if we agreed amongst ourselves, and the Government offered any assistance which they could, and which, I believe, they would gladly do, to set up – I will not say a Committee, because that is not exactly what I mean – but a representative conference, not only of parties, but of groups, a conference which would really represent opinion on these three subjects: electoral reform, revision of your electoral power when you have got it, and registration,. I believe . . . that such a conference of earnest men, holding strong views, bitterly opposed to each other, if they were face to face with these difficulties, when we are all longing with a great longing to see something of a better prospect for our country in the future, would produce an agreed system for all three questions upon which the great mass of opinion of the people of this country could come together.

He then pointed out the advantages of this approach to smoothing the passage of the reform legislation through parliament in time for the end of the war:[29]

> How easy, then, would be the work of Parliament? These differences having been removed, this Bill having been passed, the necessary legislation could be put through in a very short time, then you would, I think, once the War is over, and peace returns, have as a result of the labours of practical men a machine which would give them the power which they will be entitled to have . . . You would make them a gift, not a barren one, but a real one, and provide them also with the opportunities and the machinery by which they could record their votes, and so add to the services they have already rendered to their country by giving to it the invaluable privilege of their votes and opinions as to the future of the Empire which they have done so much to serve.

Recognizing that such a conference would need an honest broker to be set up in such a way as to carry the confidence of all parties, Walter Long offered his own services to

---

[27] Mr Winston Churchill MP remarked: 'Almost every speaker, consciously or unconsciously, avowedly or by accident, has condemned the measure for which the House is now asked to vote. The right Hon. Gentleman [Sir George Cave] himself was no exception to this general rule . . . This is what he now says to us: That Bill is an unseaworthy Bill, an illogical Bill, a bad Bill, a Bill . . . for setting up a bogus register' (Hansard, *Commons Debates*, 5th ser., lxxxv, col. 1950: 16 Aug. 1916).

[28] Hansard, *Commons Debates*, 5th ser., lxxxv, col. 1949: 16 Aug. 1916.

[29] Hansard, *Commons Debates*, 5th ser., lxxxv, col. 1949: 16 Aug. 1916.

this end. This was, indeed, better tactics than prompting the government to set up an inquiry, particularly given the precedent of the royal commission on electoral systems in 1910, whose excellent report (as so many over the century since) was shelved and consigned to oblivion.[30] Long was well-suited to the task, heading towards the end of his political career, with limited ambition to reach high office:[31]

> I believe that a conference such as I have suggested would have a great result. I hope that in the short time during which Parliament is released from its duties we shall all turn our attention to this question. If my hon. Friends in any quarter of this House, or outside of this House, were to invite me to help to get together such a conference I would do it with the utmost pleasure. I believe that is the way in which we are more likely to find a solution to these problems than any other plan of which I have heard. It was recommended by the hon. Gentleman the Member for Stockport in a speech he made, as being put forward either in public or private by many of those who have given time and attention to this question. I venture to say to the House it is our duty, one and all, not to criticise the Government or to find fault with this Bill, but to set ourselves to find a solution which may be a lasting settlement of a very old and difficult problem.

This suggestion of a conference, then, astutely lobbied for by Walter Long over the coming weeks, came to be accepted by the parliamentary parties as the best mechanism for reaching some comprehensive agreement on the many thorny issues relating to the electoral system on which resolution now had to be found.

4. *The Speaker's Conference*

There was no precedent at that time for a Speaker's conference, of which this became the first of its kind, nor any guidelines on how it should operate or, indeed, what its status was. It emerged in an *ad hoc* fashion, largely through the guiding hand of Walter Long. A politically-neutral official was needed to serve as chairman of the conference, who would play an important role in shaping its composition and terms of reference. At first it was decided to appoint a senior judicial figure as chairman, but this was scuppered by the attitude taken by the, then, lord chancellor, Lord Buckmaster, who wrote to the prime minister, Herbert Asquith, to say: 'a judge could not be spared from [the] judicial Committee for Conference on Franchise and would not be suitable anyway'.[32] Attention then turned to the one politically-neutral parliamentarian, the Speaker of the house of commons. The Speakership at that time was held by James William Lowther, later Lord Ullswater. He warmed to the task, and at the end of September was invited by the prime minister, Herbert Asquith, to chair the conference. He communicated his formal acceptance immediately prior to parliament reconvening after the summer recess on 1 October 1916.

[30] *Report of the Royal Commission on Electoral Systems*, Cd. 5163 (1910).

[31] Hansard, *Commons Debates*, 5th ser., lxxxv, cols 1949–50: 16 Aug. 1916.

[32] Bodl., Asquith Papers, xvii: Buckmaster to Asquith, 18 Sept. 1916, quoted in Martin Pugh, *Electoral Reform in War and Peace 1906–18* (1978), 72.

The membership that was assembled mainly comprised long-standing back-bench members of the Commons, with only a few senior front-bench politicians, which included Sir John Simon and Lord Salisbury. It represented a cross-section of the parliamentary parties, with some members chosen for their special knowledge of electoral affairs, such as Willoughby Dickinson.[33] At its first meeting, held on 12 October 1916 in the offices of Walter Long at the Local Government Board, the following terms of reference were adopted: 'To examine and, if possible, submit, agreed resolutions on the following matters: (a) Reform of the Franchise. (b) Basis for Redistribution of Seats. (c) Reform of the System of the Registration of Electors. (c) Method of elections and the manner in which the costs of elections should be borne.' The conference proceeded to hold 26 meetings down to its final sitting on 26 January 1917. The duration for the all-party talks and resolution of differences, therefore, took just three-and-a-half months.

Speaker Lowther was concerned not to allow meetings to get bogged down in excessive detail. His report was submitted to the prime minister the day immediately following the conference's final meeting, 27 January 1917, and consisted of an eight-page letter, listing 37 recommendations for legislative reform. This short document became the authoritative blueprint for the Representation of the People Bill. The extensive range of its recommendations covered a new system of registration of electors, enlarging the male franchise to be based on residence, granting the female suffrage, establishing a wartime register for soldiers and sailors, allowing university representation to continue, laying down rules for a redistribution of seats, stipulating all polls to be held the same day, introducing payment of a financial deposit for parliamentary candidates, and prescribing PR as the method of election in multi-member seats and the AV in single-member constituencies. The conference agreed its report unanimously, with the only area of disagreement being the female suffrage, which was approved in principle by a majority, setting out the ages of 30 and 35 years as alternatives to be considered by parliament.

5. *The Parliamentary Passage of the Bill*

By the time the conference held its final meeting, there had been a change of occupancy at 10 Downing Street, with David Lloyd George replacing Herbert Asquith on 6 December 1916 and heading a new coalition wartime government. What would now become of the Speaker's conference report? The earlier major inquiry into the electoral system had sunk without trace, the report of the royal commission on electoral systems in 1910.[34] Legislation on electoral reform needed the government's initiative to take the matter forward. In the dire national conditions prevailing, with Lloyd George more than fully occupied directing the war effort, there was a real likelihood, if not probability, that preparations for a reform bill of such great magnitude might be put off to some unspecified future date. Furthermore, there was a hard core of Unionist resistance to a reform bill in the Commons, and even more so in the house of lords.

---

[33] See *Conference on Electoral Reform, Letter from Mr Speaker to the Prime Minister*, Cd. 8463 (1917).

[34] *Report of the Royal Commission on Electoral Systems*, Cd. 5163 (1910).

Lloyd George supported legislation on the conference's recommendation, but had some initial reservations about the possible destabilising effects a reform bill might have upon the coalition and whether it might hamper his freedom of action in dissolving parliament at whatever time suited him. Any qualms he had, however, were resolved two months later by Herbert Asquith, now leader of the opposition, independently deciding to table a motion in the house of commons on the Speaker's conference report. On 28 March 1917, Mr Asquith begged to move: 'That this House records its thanks to Mr. Speaker for his services in presiding over the Electoral Reform Conference, and is of the opinion that legislation should promptly be introduced on the lines of the Resolutions reported from the Conference.'[35] Asquith's intervention in this matter was a matter of some surprise, given his well-known opposition to women's suffrage[36] and his speeches as prime minister since 1915 stating that the war precluded parliament from dealing with questions of the franchise and electoral reform. After a seven-hour debate, in which Lloyd George and Bonar Law also made speeches, the resolution in favour of a bill was passed by a surprisingly large majority, 343 ayes to 64 noes.[37] The breakdown of voting showed that support came from 188 Liberals, 79 Unionists, 51 Irish Nationalists and 24 Labour members, and the opposition was limited to 64 Unionist members. This signalled that passage of the bill was likely to be considerably less troublesome than Lloyd George and the cabinet feared.

The atmosphere and temper of a legislative chamber, shifting with events and circumstance, imposes a powerful influence on the actions taken by its members. In 1917–18, the chamber of the Commons and the general patterns of behaviour it displayed was noticeably different from the pre-war situation. This was for two main reasons, the first being that about 160 members were absent on active military service, diminishing the intensity of major debates, and meaning there was a much lower voting turnout than before and with less-predictable outcomes. The second reason was the loosened nature of party political loyalties, with divisions having opened up within the parliamentary parties and coalitions being formed across them.[38] Members were in a situation where they were controlled less by party whips than was normal. So far as government preferences on the Representation of the People Bill were concerned, the coalition cabinet decided to include the Speaker's conference's recommendations as they stood, without change, and on its two most contentious issues – those of women's suffrage and PR – to allow a free vote.

Neither did the party leaders act in a manner that sought to unduly influence back-bench members. The prime minister, Lloyd George, hardly involved himself in the parliamentary passage of the bill at all, and on the most controversial and time-consuming aspect of the bill, that of PR, he publicly declared himself agnostic. He stated in the Commons: 'I express no personal opinion upon it. I have not got any. I never made up my mind, and I really have no time to make up my mind upon it.

[35] Hansard, *Commons Debates*, 5th ser., xcii, col. 462: 28 Mar. 1917.

[36] During the debate on his motion he declared he had changed his mind on the women's suffrage: see below, pp. 44, 48.

[37] Hansard, *Commons Debates*, 5th ser., xcii, col. 566: 28 Mar. 1917.

[38] Generally, on party politics in this era, see R.C.K. Ensor, *England 1870–1914* (Oxford, 1963); Brian Harrison, *The Transformation of British Politics 1860–1995* (Oxford, 1996).

Unless I am really forced to do so, I do not propose even to study it during the War.'[39] This also meant, however, that members were less inhibited than normal about criticizing parts of the bill they did not like and in tabling amendments for consideration.

Unusually, the first reading of the bill in each House, which is normally purely formal, was the subject of some debate. In the Commons this took place under the ten minute rule procedure, with Walter Long, now elevated to secretary of state for the colonies, deputising for the home secretary, Sir George Cave, who was ill. He related the aims of the bill, explaining that: 'we have rigidly adhered to the recommendations of the conference in our preparation of the Bill'.[40] The debate on second reading, allowing an extensive debate on the general principles of the bill, clarified the battle-lines in the House, and where the main arguments for and against its provisions would lie. At the end of two days, the vote was put, with 331 members[41] voting in favour, and just 42 members against.

The committee of the whole House then scrutinised and debated the details of the legislation clause-by-clause for 23 days. By the time of the bill's report stage[42] and third reading,[43] allowing it to pass to the Lords, most of its provisions had been agreed. The two areas on which most discussion had centred was the female franchise and the method of voting, with considerable time spent also on the additional university franchise, restrictions on plural voting,[44] and the temporary disqualification of conscientious objectors from the franchise.[45]

On the female franchise, for which clause 4 of the bill provided at the age of 30 years, there had been a considerable measure of support across the political parties for many

---

[39] Hansard, *Commons Debates*, 5th ser., xcii, col. 492: 28 Mar. 1917. From personal conversations recorded by his friend, C.P. Scott, editor of the *Manchester Guardian*, in *The Political Diaries of C. P. Scott 1911–1928*, ed. Trevor Wilson (1970), Lloyd George's private views on PR appear to have been erratic. On 28 Jan. 1917 Scott records him saying he would support PR 'all round or not at all' (259); but then on 3 Apr. 1917 Lloyd George argued with Scott who favoured PR, saying it was 'a device for defeating democracy' and would bring 'faddists of all kind into Parliament' (274). After leaving office, Lloyd George regretted that he had not implemented PR, and is quoted in Scott's diary entry for 13–14 Nov. 1925 saying: 'Someone ought to have come to me in 1918 and gone into the whole matter. I was not converted then. I could have carried it then when I was prime minister' (485).

[40] Hansard, *Commons Debates*, 5th ser., xciii, col. 1493: 15 May 1917.

[41] Of those voting in favour of the second reading, the Liberal and Labour vote remained similar and the Unionist support rose to 110. The reduced number of votes from the earlier debate on 28 March was due to abstentions by Irish Nationalists. The 42 noes were cast by Unionists.

[42] Hansard, *Commons Debates*, 5th ser., xcix, cols 613–730, 1035–152, 1209–325, 1406–520, 1673–799, 2060–179, 2277–448: 15, 20, 21, 22, 26, 28, 29 Nov. 1917 respectively.

[43] Hansard, *Commons Debates*, 5th ser., c, cols 265–382, 456–572, 677–795, 819–28: 4, 5, 6, 7 Dec. 1917 respectively.

[44] Abolition of plural voting had been a Liberal policy for many years. It was known that most electors entitled to more than one vote under the pre-existing law were Conservatives. In 1906 a bill to abolish plural voting had been presented to parliament by the Liberal government and passed the house of commons, but had been rejected by the house of lords.

[45] Section 9(2), which disqualified conscientious objectors for five years. This provision was not in the original bill and was inserted after an amendment moved by Ronald MacNeill in the house of commons, who said: 'I have very little doubt that a great many of them are sincere, and I have very little doubt that a large number of them are insincere. But in that respect one cannot divide the sheep from the goats': see Hansard, *Commons Debates*, 5th ser., xcv, cols 307–8: 26 June 1917.

years. However, substantial resistance remained,[46] and senior figures in the previous cabinets had been reluctant to resolve the issue or bring forward legislation. Herbert Asquith, the former prime minister, had been well known for his opposition, so it was with great public interest that in 1917 he announced to the Commons that he had changed his mind on the subject. He set out his reasons for doing so, as follows:[47]

> I am glad to have the opportunity to disclose the process which has operated on my mind. My opposition to woman suffrage has always been based, and based solely, on considerations of public expediency. I think that some years ago I ventured to use the expression, 'Let the women work out their own salvation.' Well, Sir, they have worked it out during this War. How could we have carried on the War without them? Short of actually bearing arms in the field, there is hardly a service which had contributed, or is contributing, to the maintenance of our cause in which women have not been at least as active and as efficient as men, and wherever we turn we see them doing, with zeal and success . . . work which three years ago would have been regarded as falling exclusively within the province of men. This is not a merely sentimental argument, though it appeals to our feelings as well as our judgment. But what I confess moves me still more in this matter is the problem of reconstruction when the War is over. The questions which will then necessarily arise in regard to women's labour and women's functions and activities in the new ordering of things – for, do not doubt it, the old order will be changed – are questions in regard to which I, for my part, feel it impossible, consistently either with justice or with expediency, to withhold from women the power and the right of making their voice directly heard.

His views reflected the shift in opinion that had taken place across the House. He also made positive reference to the suffragettes having refrained for three years during the course of the war from their notorious programme of public disruption, self-harm, and terrorist activities, which in many quarters had served to damage the cause of women's suffrage and stiffen opposition among politicians who were determined not to give in to such threats of violence. As Asquith said: 'And let me add that, since the War began, now nearly three years ago, we have had no recurrence of that detestable campaign which disfigured the annals of political agitation in this country, and no one can now contend that we are yielding to violence.'[48]

The original version of the Representation of the People Bill[49] followed the confer-ence's recommendations on new methods of voting to replace the traditional simple plurality system. This, as mentioned above, was for PR in constituencies having three or

---

[46] Official party views on the subject did not exist. Among the ranks of the Labour movement, in 1912 a resolution was passed at the annual conference on franchise reform requesting the parliamentary party:'to make it clear that no bill can be acceptable to the Labour and Socialist Movement which does not include women' (R. Miliband, *Parliamentary Socialism* (2nd edn, 1972), 24). However, at the party conference on 20 Mar. 1917 a motion for 'complete adult suffrage' seconded by Miss Sylvia Pankhurst was lost on a card vote by 2,662,000 to 88,000, and an amendment calling for the enfranchisement of women 'on the same basis as men' was also lost (*The Times*, 21 Mar. 1917).

[47] Hansard, *Commons Debates*, 5th ser., xcii, col. 469: 28 Mar. 1917.

[48] Hansard, *Commons Debates*, 5th ser., xcii, col. 470: 28 Mar. 1917.

[49] HC Bill 125.

more members, using the single transferable vote; and in single-member constituencies, the AV. It was these proposals that proved the most contentious aspect of the bill within the house of commons, and in disagreements between the Commons and the Lords.

To some extent, the case for PR had already been damaged in the arrangements for setting up the Boundary Commissions taking place earlier in the year. The three commissions for England and Wales, Scotland, and Ireland were established by warrant of the home, Scottish, and Irish secretaries of state[50] to review and determine the boundaries of parliamentary constituencies and the number of members assigned to each, in readiness for their recommendations to be included in the Representation of the People Bill which was about to be introduced. However, the terms of reference of the English commission were subsequently varied on 22 June 1917, following a resolution of the house of commons on 18 June, to the effect that: 'the Commissioners shall act on the assumption that proportional representation is not adopted'.[51] This had only narrowly passed, with voting on the resolution being 149 ayes to 141 noes.

The rationale for the method of election in the government bill was explained by the home secretary in his presentation of the bill at second reading. There was PR to ensure that significant minorities in the larger constituencies, ones returning two or more members, would not be wholly excluded from representation in the house of commons.[52] The object, he said, 'was not to protect majorities against loss of representation, but to protect minorities against total elimination'. The rationale for the AV method in the single-member constituencies was that elected members should obtain a majority of votes cast in a constituency. 'The object of that provision', Sir George Cave told the House, 'is to prevent what has happened from time to time, the possibility of a candidate who represents a minority only of voters being elected because the votes of the majority are split between two other candidates.'[53]

Various arguments of principle were produced for and against adoption of the scheme of voting proposed. However, a powerful determining factor was the vested interest of a great many members in retaining the existing single-member constituencies to avoid having their own constituency boundary redrawn and having to compete against other members in newly-created, larger voting areas. During the committee stage in August, amendments on the method of election were tabled and PR was defeated, with the AV being put in its place in the electoral areas affected.[54] This was carried by a single vote, 126 to 125. At report stage, the AV was, again, endorsed in place of PR in a vote taken in the House,[55] by 150 to 121 votes, subject to retention of the single transferable vote as the method of election in the university constituencies. Thus, although the Speaker's conference had unanimously endorsed PR, the house of commons voted it down three times in favour of the AV.

A major struggle with the house of lords, however, was now to commence. The second chamber devoted seven weeks to the amended bill, returning it to the lower

---

[50] Cd. 8576 (14 May 1917), Cd. 8585 (16 May 1917), Cd. 8919 (19 Jan. 1918) respectively.

[51] *Letter Amending Instructions in Accordance with Resolution of the House of Commons*, Cd. 8670 (1917).

[52] Sir George Cave: Hansard, *Commons Debates*, 5th ser., xciii, col. 2139: 22 May 1917.

[53] Hansard, *Commons Debates*, 5th ser., xciii, col. 2138: 22 May 1917.

[54] Hansard, *Commons Debates*, 5th ser., xcvii, cols 605–704: 9 Aug. 1917.

[55] Hansard, *Commons Debates*, 5th ser., xcix, cols 1406–502: 22 Nov. 1917.

House on 30 January 1918 with the AV deleted from its provisions, and PR reinstated in constituencies returning between three and five members.[56] After an 11-hour debate on the method of election, the Commons voted to disagree with these Lords' amendments, by 223 votes to 113.[57] The reason given to the Lords was: 'Because they consider it undesirable to apply the principle of proportional representation, especially in view of the delay which would be caused thereby to the passage of the Bill.' In the single-member constituencies, they reinserted the AV: 'because they desire to adhere to the principle of the alternative vote'.

By now the issue had acquired a higher public profile than ever before. In January, the Labour Party endorsed PR as its official policy at its annual conference. The topic was also subject to considerable press coverage, for example the *Manchester Guardian* lobbying in support of the house of lords' stand, stating:[58]

> The Lords are not alone. They have powerful backing, and as they happen in this matter to be right and to be sustaining a more democratic principle than their opponents they will have whatever advantage may belong to those who have the better cause . . . The fact is that the Lords are, in this matter, fulfilling the true function of a Second Chamber by giving to the popular House an opportunity of reconsideration where reconsideration is clearly needed.

When the bill returned to the second chamber for reconsideration on 4 February, the Lords once again rejected the AV, sending a message to the Commons that this was: 'Because in their view the adoption of the alternative vote would introduce serious complexities into the electoral system without any corresponding advantage', and they insisted on PR, though with more limited application across the country. The following day, the Commons once again disagreed with the Lords' amendment, sending their message to the Lords saying this was: 'Because they consider the partial application of proportional representation as now proposed by the Lords is open to at least as much objection as the original proposal, and they are therefore unwilling to adopt it, especially in view of the strong objections which have been expressed by the representatives of some of the principal constituencies affected.' The Commons also reinstated the AV, but this time in the narrowest of votes with the majority reduced to just one, 195 to 194.[59]

The bill was returned to the house of lords for the third time on 6 February 1918, with the end of the session and prorogation ceremony scheduled for later the same day. If an agreement was not reached, the whole bill would be lost. A flurry of negotiations and messages of agreement and disagreement between the two Houses took place, resulting in an agreed compromise, in which the AV was dropped, and the application of PR restricted to a royal commission being set up to prepare a limited experimental scheme of PR to submit. The act was given the royal assent later that day and passed into law.

[56] See the report stage: Hansard, *Lords Debates*, 5th ser., xxvii, cols 1236–40: 28 Jan. 1918.

[57] Hansard, *Commons Debates*, 5th ser., ci, col. 1704: 30 Jan. 1918.

[58] 28 Jan. 1918.

[59] Hansard, *Commons Debates*, 5th ser., xxx, col. 2198: 5 Feb. 1918.

Two months later, on 13 April, the royal commission arising from the compromise published its scheme of PR, which would affect 99 members across 24 newly-enlarged constituencies.[60] It was debated in the house of commons the following month, and quietly rejected.[61]

Perhaps the 'hands off' approach of the government on the issue of PR and the AV, with members allowed a free vote, was a wise approach from the point of view of piloting a complete bill onto the statute book. Lloyd George did state that he believed the Speaker's conference would not have wished to imperil the rest of their recommendations by pressing their proposals for PR – it was not, he said, 'an essential part' of their package and programme for reform.[62] Had the government been determined on the matter, it could have swayed opinion in the Commons. Regarding the house of lords' rejection of the AV, a government resolved on supporting this reform might have taken a more threatening posture against the Lords, particularly with reform of its constitution being then under review by the royal commission on the future of the second chamber.

6. *Lessons and Consequences of the Act*

In addition to the practical reforms it brought to the British system of voting and elections, the Representation of the People Act 1918 was a symbolic measure of immense significance to the constitution. It consecrated the principle of political equality in British political life, and settled arguments that had raged within the 19th-century establishment about the wisdom and effects of allowing the masses to choose their masters. People could now say they lived in a democracy, albeit one still shrouded in a deeply-ingrained social class system. As noted above, the momentum created by directly admitting women into political life led to the reduction in their voting age to 21 years, in parity with men, ten years later by the Parliament (Qualification of Women) Act 1928.

Some significant lessons and precedents were learnt from this particular item of constitutional legislation and on how such an ambitious and controversial programme of changes could be resolved politically and carried though to the statute book. First, in the politics of constitutional reform, personalities matter. A great deal of credit for getting the Representation of the People Bill on the statute book must go to David Lloyd George. This may seem a surprising suggestion at first, for as discussed above, the prime minister was noticeably absent in the parliamentary debates on the bill, leaving it to his cabinet colleagues, especially the home secretary, Sir George Cave, to pilot the bill through parliament. But the reality of any major constitutional reform is that strong leadership, of whatever kind, must come from 10 Downing Street – and certainly nothing without its endorsement will pass into law. As Martin Pugh has written: 'The credit due to him

---

[60] *Report of the Royal Commission on a Scheme for Proportional Representation*, Cd. 9044 (1918).

[61] Hansard, *Commons Debates*, 5th ser., cvi, cols 63–117: 13 May 1918. The voting on the resolution to approve was 110 ayes to 166 noes. It was then resolved: 'That, in the opinion of this House, the change in the method of Parliamentary representation and elections involved in the adoption of the Report is inadvisable, that the scheme is not justified by the nature and extent or the results of the local inquiries held; and that the House declines to proceed further in the matter.'

[62] Hansard, *Commons Debates*, 5th ser., xcii, col. 492: 28 Mar. 1917.

is that for taking the initiative and pushing out the venture; after that he left the work
to others in the belief that the details were less important than the fact of the Bill itself.'[63]
The prime minister had the mental energy and political resolve to support and push the
legislation along from 10 Downing Street, whilst not allowing himself to be deflected
(and criticized for being deflected) in his primary duties in overseeing the war effort.

The motion to adopt the conference's report put forward by Herbert Asquith in the
Commons[64] proved fortuitous, if not essential, to the reform. The complex relationship
between Lloyd George as prime minister and Asquith, the former colleague whom he
ousted as prime minister and who then became leader of the opposition, caused a train
of events that proved beneficial to the prospects of the bill. Asquith as prime minister had
not wanted to touch electoral reform. He buried the report of the royal commission on
electoral systems in 1910, and during the war made clear his opposition to legislation to
reform the franchise in several speeches to parliament. In August 1916, for example,
he said:[65]

> It seems to me, and it seems to all my colleagues – although I do not profess for a
> moment that we are in agreement on all these points as to whom ought or ought not
> to be enfranchise – that nothing would be more injurious to the best interests of the
> country, nothing more damaging to the prosecution of the War, nothing more fatal to
> the concentration of the national effort, than that the floodgates should be opened on
> all those vast, complicated questions of the franchise, with an infinite multiplicity of
> claimants, each of whom can make a perfectly plausible if not irresistible case for
> themselves, and that at this stage of the war that that should be thrown on the floor
> of the House of Commons, and into the arena of public discussion outside, and that
> we should be diverted from that which ought to be our supreme and sole purpose to
> what is practically a review of the whole basis of our electoral constitution.

Why, then, was it Asquith who put forward the motion that the government should
bring forward legislation on franchise and electoral reform a year later in the House?[66]
Had he undergone a conversion of opinion; was he now shamed in not having dealt
with these such important issues when he had ample opportunity to do so during his
seven-year premiership; was it a device to stymie a dissolution of parliament that year
believing his Liberal group of members would be decimated at the polls;[67] or was he
attempting to embarrass Lloyd George by foisting upon him, through a parliamentary
vote, a legislative task he believed impossibly ambitious and would end in either political

[63] Pugh, *Electoral Reform in War and Peace 1906–18*, p. 89.

[64] See above, p. 42.

[65] Hansard, *Commons Debates*, 5th ser., lxxxv, col. 1451: 14 Aug. 1916. In another speech the previous year,
he said: 'All our efforts and our energies as a people are concentrated upon the War . . . It would not only be
idle, but I think it would be offensive to the good sense of the nation to proceed at such a time with
controversial legislation or with the more or less academic discussion of possible social and political reforms':
Hansard, *Commons Debates*, 5th ser., lxix, cols 46–7: 3 Feb. 1915.

[66] See above, p. 42.

[67] Credence for this factor influencing Asquith can be gleaned from the rather exaggerated language he used
during the debate of 28 Mar. 1917 on his motion for legislation on the Speaker's conference report, when he
argued that a general election that year would be an 'absurdity': Hansard, *Commons Debates*, 5th ser., xcii, col.
463.

disaster or embarrassment for the prime minister? Whatever Asquith's true motives – and they may well have been a mixture of all four – in the event he contributed to perhaps the only true liberal achievement of Lloyd George's premiership.

Although precedents existed for informal all-party talks on constitutional legislation, including those taking place prior to the Representation of the People Acts in 1884–5,[68] the idea of harnessing the Speaker as chairman of the conference in 1916–17 was regarded as so successful as to entrench itself as a procedural model for future all-party talks on difficult electoral matters. Speaker Lowther himself was called upon to chair two further conferences, in 1919–20 on devolution, and (after his retirement) in 1929–30 on PR and the AV, though neither of these led to changes in the law.

However, the conference of 1916–17 was followed as an almost exact precedent in 1944, also at a time of war, and also after a period of successive prolongations of parliament, in examining the redistribution of seats and reform of the franchise, conduct and costs of elections, and methods of election. In helping set up the conference, Herbert Morrison, the, then, home secretary, explained to the house of commons:[69]

> We propose that it shall be substantially as it was before. We propose that a letter should be sent by the Prime Minister to you, Mr Speaker, asking you to preside over the Conference . . . The Speaker's Conference, which will represent all political parties as far as practicable, will itself agree on the principles of redistribution, and the directions to the boundary commissioners, and if they do I shall be very grateful. It will save me a nasty job, an invidious job, and I think it is the way it should be done. The political parties should get round the table under Mr Speaker and try amicably and fairly to settle the principles on which they should act.

Its reports[70] led to the Representation of the People Act 1944, removing the period of residency required, plural voting, and the business and university franchises. The House of Commons (Redistribution of Seats) Act 1944 established a permanent machinery of independent Boundary Commissions for future redistributions of parliamentary seats, operating under the supervisory chairmanship of the Speaker.[71]

Subsequently, there have been five Speaker's conferences, all concerned with issues of parliamentary representation. In 1965–8, Speaker Hylton-Foster, then Speaker King, presided over all-party talks on the voting age, electoral registration, method and conduct of elections, election expenses, the use of broadcasting, and election petitions. In agreeing to chair the conference, Speaker Hylton-Foster told the Commons that the review was directly following the precedents of 1916 and 1944.[72] Its report made 71 recommendations, 60 of which were accepted by the home secretary, James Callaghan, on behalf of the government.[73] During the next decade, in 1973–4 Speaker Selwyn Lloyd chaired a

---

[68] See David Rolf, 'Origins of Mr Speaker's Conference During the First World War', *History*, lxiv (1979), 36–46.

[69] Hansard, *Commons Debates*, 5th ser., cccxcvi, cols 1166, 1160: 10 Feb. 1944.

[70] *Conference on Electoral Machinery and Redistribution of Seats*, Cmds 6534, 6543 (1944).

[71] The legislation has been further amended since, and was consolidated with amendments in the Parliamentary Constituencies Act 1986. See Blackburn, *The Electoral System in Britain*, ch. 4.

[72] Hansard, *Commons Debates*, 5th ser., dccxii, col. 520: 12 May 1965.

[73] Hansard, *Commons Debates*, 5th ser., dcclxix, col. 576: 24 July 1968.

conference on electoral registration,[74] and in 1977–8 Speaker Thomas chaired a conference to consider the number of parliamentary constituencies in Northern Ireland.[75] After
30 years, in 2009 this consensus-seeking mechanism was again utilised on the initiative
of the prime minister, to examine and bring forward recommendations on female and
ethnic minority representation, and on whether the voting age should be reduced to 16
years and weekend voting should be introduced.[76]

Radical reforms in peacetime, certainly on the constitution, have almost always had
to be driven through parliament in the teeth of opposition. None the less, the health
of the political system in the 20th century, and its ability to agree on fundamentals
when the occasion demands, was evident in the response of parliamentarians to
embrace national coalitions during the two most dire emergencies of the century,
during the First World War and the Second World War. No doubt many of the
changes wrought by the Representation of the People Act 1918 would have come to
pass in the years to follow, but its precise timing owed a great deal to this search for
common ground engendered by the war. As Speaker Lowther testified:[77]

> I should like to bear witness to the admirable temper and conciliatory disposition
> which all the members of the Conference showed in grappling with the difficulties
> confronting them. They were convinced, I feel sure, of the great desirability of
> amicably settling these thorny questions, and of finding a solution for issues fraught
> with the possibility of engendering grave domestic strife and internal friction. They
> were desirous of rendering, at a time when the national energies were almost wholly
> centred upon the successful prosecution of the war, a service which might prove of
> the highest value to the State, and result in equipping the nation with a truly
> representative House of Commons, capable of dealing, and dealing effectively, with
> the many and gigantic problems which it will have to face and solve as soon as the
> restoration of peace permits of their calm and dispassionate consideration.

The wider effects of the act were far-reaching, and indirectly served to recalibrate the
relationships and functioning of almost every part of the constitutional structure. It
elevated the popular authority of the house of commons in its balance of power with the
second chamber. The extent to which universal suffrage contributed to Labour's success
in usurping the former position of the Liberal Party as the progressive party of the left
is debateable, but clearly Labour's grass-roots organisations and trade union association
played some significant role in capturing the newly-enfranchised working-class votes. In
constitutional ideology, universal suffrage promoted a doctrine of the mandate whereby
governments came to justify their actions more forcefully by reference to items of policy

---

[74] *Conference on Electoral Law*, Cmnds 5363, 5469, 5500, 5547 (1974), leading to the Representation of the
People Act 1974.

[75] *Conference on Electoral Law, Letter from Mr Speaker to the Prime Minister*, Cmnd. 7110 (1978).

[76] For the Speaker's announcement of the conference's proposed terms of reference, see Hansard, *Commons
Debates*, 6th ser., cdlxxix, col. 659: 22 July 2008; and for the house of commons' resolution on the conference,
see Hansard, *Commons Debates*, 6th ser., cdlxxxii, col. 912: 12 Nov. 2008.

[77] *Conference on Electoral Reform, Letter from Mr Speaker to the Prime Minister*, Cd. 8463 (1917), 8.

contained in their previous election manifestos, however dubious on other constitutional or moral grounds the proposed measure might be.[78]

But the greatest consequence of the act arose from the house of commons' decision not to adopt the Speaker's conference recommendations on PR. The legacy of the 1884–5 reforms, discussed above, bringing in a majority of single-member constituencies, had been to leave too many members in the Commons facing loss of their seat or a serious inconvenience through a radical boundary review to feel able to support it. Time and again throughout the 20th century it has been shown that, at key moments in our constitutional history, politicians will act and vote consistently with their vested self-interests, with only a few puritans and those about to retire acting genuinely in accordance with their best constitutional judgment and conscience. What amounted by default to endorsement of the simple plurality (or first-past-the-post) system of elections had a profound consequence on the operation of parliamentary democracy for the rest of the 20th century.

First-past-the-post voting tends towards the least number of political parties in a legislature, diminishing or excluding altogether the presence of third and minority parties. In Britain, it has shaped a two-party domination of the parliamentary process and a sharply adversarial culture in political discourse. By producing an exaggerated majority of seats in the house of commons for the largest party,[79] the voting system has allowed the executive to dominate parliament to a much greater extent than would otherwise have been likely under PR. This, in turn, has had an outcome in terms of national social policy pursued by whatever government is in office.[80] Some have argued that because in the early part of the 20th century the centre-left became fragmented into two parties (Labour and Liberals/Liberal Democrats), the centre-right (Conservatives) have been able to take office on occasions when, under a proportional method of election, they would have been unable to do so.[81] There would have been more frequent occasions of coalition government or legislative pacts under a minority government (such as those between Labour and the Liberals in 1977–8), fostering greater continuity in public policy.

The Representation of the People Act settled many democratic aspects of the nation's modern electoral system, most notably the universal suffrage, but controversy over the most appropriate method of electing members in the Commons continued to flare up at periodic intervals over the course of the 20th century. In 1929–31, only the financial crisis and collapse of the minority Labour administration prevented the AV from being adopted.[82] In the 1980s, the political shooting star of the Social Democratic Party and

[78] For discussion of this as 'false political doctrine' by a long-serving lord chancellor (1970–4, 1979–87) see Lord Hailsham, *The Dilemma of Democracy* (1978), ch. 20.

[79] For instance, in Tony Blair's electoral triumph in 1977, with Labour taking 419 (or 63.6%) of the 659 seats in the Commons, only 43.2% of votes cast for Labour.

[80] For an exposition on this point by a former senior cabinet minister, see Roy Jenkins, *Home Thoughts from Abroad* (Richard Dimbleby Lecture, 1979).

[81] Generally, see David Marquand, *The Progressive Dilemma: From Lloyd George to Blair* (1999). On voting statistics, see Blackburn, *The Electoral System in Britain*, chs 1, 8. E.g., in 1979 when Margaret Thatcher formed her first administration with an overall majority of 43 her Conservative Party only polled 43.9% of the vote, whereas Labour and the Liberals combined polled a majority (51.7%).

[82] For an account, see D. Butler, *The Electoral System in Britain since 1918* (2nd edn, Oxford, 1962); and V. Bogdanor, *The People and the Party System* (Cambridge, 1981).

Liberal Alliance and the reform group Charter '88 succeeded in making PR again a major public issue of debate.[83] In 1997 the Labour government took office with a manifesto commitment to establish a commission on the voting system to recommend 'a proportional alternative' to the first-past-the-post method of electing the Commons, which would then be put to a popular referendum. The commission was duly established and reported its conclusions in 1998, recommending a mixed system of the AV plus additional party list members.[84] However, comfortable with its large majority in the Commons, the government under Tony Blair then reneged on its promise and decided not to hold a referendum after all.

At the 2009 Labour Party conference, the then prime minister, Gordon Brown, once again committed Labour to a referendum on the electoral system, assuming it won the 2010 general election. This time the promise was limited to offering the AV as a new basis for elections. This would be supported by the Liberal Democrats, whose support Mr Brown would need to remain in office if the 2010 election resulted in a hung parliament, even though its own party preference for many years has been for the single transferable vote. The Conservatives continued to oppose any change in the method of election, but following the indecisive results of the 2010 general election, entered into negotiations with the Liberal Democrats in order to form a coalition. A consequence was an agreement to hold a referendum on the use of the AV for parliamentary elections. Both parties committed themselves to the referendum but agreed that members would be free to argue on whichever side they wished. For many Conservatives the AV was a step too far and for many Liberal Democrats one that fell short of what was desirable. The most appropriate electoral system for electing members of parliament may never be conclusively settled to the satisfaction of all. The debate experienced in 1918 has continued to the present day.

[83] See, e.g., Liberal/SDP Commission, *Electoral Reform: Fairer Voting in Natural Communities* (1982); and for a contemporary discussion, P. Norton, 'Does Britain Need Proportional Representation?', in *Constitutional Studies*, ed. R. Blackburn (1992), ch. 9.

[84] *The Report of the Independent Commission on the Voting System*, Cm. 4090 (1998).

Divided Loyalties:
The European Communities Act 1972

PHILIP NORTON

UK membership of the European Communities (EC) was prompted by economic and political factors. It represented a novel constitutional departure; one that was contested. The proposal for membership created divisions between, and within, both main parties. Although both Houses voted overwhelmingly in support of the principle of the membership, the short bill to give legal effect in UK law to membership was bitterly contested, the government achieving the second reading of the bill through a vote of confidence. The bill was opposed consistently by the Labour opposition and dissident Conservative back benchers, though passage of the bill was achieved eventually, courtesy of Liberals and some abstaining Labour MPs, and without amendment. The act enabled the United Kingdom to become a member of the EC, with important consequences for the UK constitution, including creating a juridical dimension unparalleled since before the Glorious Revolution of 1688. Parliament has provided for its own legislation to be subordinate to that of the EC, while adapting to the new situation through the creation of committees to scrutinise European documents.

Keywords: European Economic Community (EEC); European Communities (EC); European Communities Bill; house of commons; house of lords; Labour Party; Conservative Party; legislation

Membership of the European Communities (EC) was one of the most politically-contentious issues in British politics in the last half of the 20th century. The issue caused deep rifts within, as well as between, political parties. Both main political parties shifted their stance on the issue and each had difficulty in carrying its parliamentary supporters with it. The European Communities Bill incorporated the changes necessary in domestic law to give effect to UK membership of the EC. The passage of the bill was tortuous and its consequences, not least in constitutional terms, not well appreciated.

The EC comprised the European Coal and Steel Community (ECSC), the European Atomic Energy Community (Euratom) and the European Economic Community (EEC). The ECSC had been formed in 1951 under the Treaty of Paris and the other two communities were created in 1958 under the Treaty of Rome. The three communities had merged in 1967. There were six member states: Germany, France, Italy and the Benelux countries. The UK had declined to participate in the negotiation of the treaties. Winston Churchill put the case for Britain to engage in the Paris talks but his motion in support of participation was defeated in the house of commons by a majority of 20. Churchill's successor as Conservative leader, Sir Anthony Eden, and Clement Attlee's successor as Labour leader, Hugh Gaitskell, were both opposed to taking part in the talks leading to the Treaty of Rome.

The imperatives for the UK to participate in the moves towards European integration were not as profound as in the case of its continental neighbours.[1] The UK still saw itself as a world power, it had a Commonwealth, and it had stood alone as an island nation for centuries. The other countries of western Europe appeared in a worse shape economically and politically than did Britain. The country enjoyed relative economic prosperity in the 1950s. There seemed little incentive to participate. Conservatives did not want to jeopardise the freedom of the British government to act on the world stage: the nation had a status not enjoyed by other European states. The Labour Party was wary of a body that could limit the policy goals of a socialist government.

The situation changed at the end of the 1950s as the nation faced political and economic problems. Britain's role as an independent world actor was in question. It had lost an empire. The Commonwealth comprised nations able to pursue policies independent of the UK. The USA was now the dominant world power and Britain's influence with it not as great as British ministers may have wished. The cancellation of the Blue Streak rocket in 1960 highlighted Britain's dependence on its transatlantic ally. Economic conditions worsened. The Commonwealth was not proving to be the source of trade that many politicians had anticipated. The EEC started to look attractive, boosting a growth rate that outstripped that of the UK. It also began to look attractive from a political perspective, offering the potential for the United Kingdom to regain a leadership role on the international stage. The economic and political advantages were seen as linked, a point variously made by Conservative prime minister, Harold Macmillan, both to US president, John Kennedy[2] and to parliament. 'Although the Treaty of Rome is concerned with economic matters, it has an important political objective', he declared, 'namely to promote unity and stability in Europe . . . In this modern world the tendency towards larger groups of nations acting together in the common interest leads to greater unity and thus adds to our strength in the struggle for freedom.'[3]

The USA indicated its preference for the UK to join the EC. Under Macmillan's premiership, a clear shift in thinking occurred within the British government and on 31 July 1961, Macmillan announced to the house of commons that Britain was applying for membership of the EEC. The decision was debated in a two-day debate on 2–3 August. An opposition amendment, moved by Hugh Gaitskell, stipulating the need for approval by the Commonwealth prime ministers' conference and for conditions of membership to be compatible with the UK's obligations to its European Free Trade Area (EFTA) partners, was defeated by 318 votes to 209. The government motion, approving the decision, was then agreed by 313 votes to five.[4] According to *The Times*, 24 Conservative MPs abstained from voting in the first division and 29 in the second.[5]

The application for membership failed not because of the British parliament but because of the actions of the French president. Charles de Gaulle vetoed the application, fearing that the UK was too tied to the USA. In 1967, a second application was made, this time by the Labour government under Harold Wilson, reflecting a change of

[1] See Anthony King, *Britain Says Yes* (Washington, 1977), 2–7.
[2] Miriam Camps, *Britain and the European Community 1955–1963* (Oxford, 1964), 336.
[3] Quoted in Edward Heath, *The Course of My Life* (1998), 210.
[4] Hansard, *Commons Debates*, 5th ser., dcxlv, cols 1781–4: 3 Aug. 1961.
[5] *The Times*, 4 Aug. 1961.

thinking within Labour's ranks.[6] (At a meeting at Chequers, cabinet ministers had voted 13 to eight in favour of an unconditional application.)[7] Wilson told the Commons that membership would create a new confidence in British industry and provide a greater emphasis on modernisation and productivity as well as impart a new dynamic to the community. Following a three-day debate, a back-bench Conservative amendment, moved by Robin Turton, MP for Thirsk and Malton, regretting the government's decision, was lost by 487 votes to 26. A motion approving the government's white paper on membership, supported by both the government and opposition, was approved by 488 votes to 62.[8] Thirty-six Labour and 26 Conservative MPs voted against the motion; 50 Labour MPs abstained from voting.[9]

In 1969, de Gaulle resigned as president of France – to be replaced by Georges Pompidou, more sympathetic to British membership – and formal agreement to open negotiations was reached. A general election intervened and a Conservative government under Edward Heath was returned in June 1970 with an overall majority of 33. The Conservative manifesto expressed the view that, if the right terms could be negotiated, it would be in the long-term interest of the UK to join the EEC.

Negotiations opened on 30 June 1970 and by October of the following year most of the terms had been agreed. Following a debate in the Commons in July 1971, the government recommended entry on the terms negotiated. In October, the Commons held a six-day debate on a motion to approve the government's 'decision of principle to join the European Communities on the basis of the arrangements which have been negotiated'. One-hundred-and-eighty MPs took part.[10] The opposition, though remaining in favour of membership in principle, opposed membership on the terms negotiated. Denis Healey argued that adverse economic conditions meant it would be difficult to meet the foreign exchange burdens resulting from the terms negotiated. It would require deflation or devaluation. A number of Conservative back benchers spoke against the motion and several Labour MPs supported it. William Rodgers, Labour MP for Stockton-on-Tees, argued that they could not expect better terms in the future. The government allowed a free vote, whereas the opposition imposed a three-line whip. The motion was carried by 356 votes to 244, a government majority of 112. There were 39 Conservative MPs in the opposition lobby, but they were more than offset by 69 Labour MPs who voted for the motion. A further 20 Labour MPs, and two Conservatives, abstained from voting.[11] The vote was the high point of parliamentary support for membership of the EC.

The government achieved a success early in 1972 when the opposition tabled a motion calling upon the government not to sign the treaty of accession until the full text had been published and its contents laid before the House. The government tabled an amendment which noted that that the treaty would not become operative until ratified and approved the government's intention to lay before the House the full and agreed

[6] See Uwe Kitzinger, *The Second Try* (Oxford, 1968).

[7] Tony Benn, *Out of the Wilderness: Diaries 1963–67* (1988), 496.

[8] Hansard, *Commons Debates*, 5th ser., dccxlvi, cols 1645–56: 10 May 1967.

[9] Philip Norton, *Dissension in the House of Commons 1945–74* (1975), 271–2. The voting figures include the tellers. Two other MPs opposed the motion.

[10] Uwe Kitzinger, *Diplomacy and Persuasion* (1973), 371.

[11] Norton, *Dissension in the House of Commons 1945–74*, pp. 397–8.

text when signed as well as details of the government's intentions for legislation. The amendment was carried by 298 votes to 277. Four Conservatives voted against and 17 abstained, the 17 remaining in the chamber while the vote took place; two Labour MPs abstained. The motion as amended was then carried by 296 votes to 276, with the same MPs dissenting from the party line.[12] The government victory led *The Times* to claim that: 'there is no doubt that the Conservative anti-Market group has collapsed.'[13] It was not long before it was claiming the opposite.

1. *The Passage of the Bill*[14]

In order to reduce the potential for lengthy debates on the bill, the government opted for a short bill. Given a choice between a blockbuster bill amending all relevant legislation affected by entry – likely to absorb an inordinate amount of parliamentary time – and a one-clause enabling bill, the government moved very much in the direction of the latter. It was designed, wrote Edward Heath, 'so as to balance our wish for tight legislation not open to attack with the need for a proper debate on the issues.'[15] The solicitor general, Sir Geoffrey Howe, and the senior parliamentary counsel, Sir John Fiennes, produced a bill of 12 clauses and four schedules, covering 37 pages. As Howe was to record: 'In retrospect, that was the easy part. It was the parliamentary handling that was to test us more severely.'[16] Second reading of the European Communities Bill in the house of commons was scheduled for 17 February 1972.

The three-day debate on second reading reflected the divisions, especially within the government's ranks. There was intense activity by the whips: 'the three-line whips cracked with no concessions to conscience', recalled new MP, Norman Tebbit.[17] In some cases, constituency parties were active in pressing anti-EEC MPs to support the government: of the 39 Conservative MPs to vote against EC entry in the October 1971 vote, 21 encountered some constituency pressure.[18] Despite this intense activity, it was not certain that the government would win the vote. Labour MPs were under pressure to oppose the bill, especially given that the vote would be whipped on both sides. Labour supporters of the EEC reluctantly went along with the leadership.[19] As a result, the prime minister announced that the vote was to be one of confidence: if the vote was lost, the government would resign. This was designed to maximise Conservative support in the lobbies. It also had the effect of reducing the likelihood of Labour MPs supporting the government.

[12] Hansard, *Commons Debates*, 5th ser., dcccxxix, cols 799–810: 20 Jan. 1972. See also *The Times*, 21 Jan. 1972, which recorded the names of those who abstained. Norton, *Dissension in the House of Commons 1945–74*, pp. 402–3.

[13] *The Times*, 21 Jan. 1972.

[14] This section draws heavily on research previously carried out by the author: Philip Norton, *Conservative Dissidents* (1978), 64–82.

[15] Heath, *The Course of My Life*, 383.

[16] Geoffrey Howe, *Conflict of Loyalty* (1994), 68.

[17] Norman Tebbitt, *Upwardly Mobile* (1989), 149.

[18] See Norton, *Conservative Dissidents*, 177–91.

[19] See David Owen, *Time to Declare* (1991), 186–7.

In opening the debate, the minister responsible for the negotiations, chancellor of the duchy of Lancaster, Geoffrey Rippon, explained that the bill was consequential on the provisions of the treaty of accession and was a necessary preliminary to its ratification and coming into operation. It made changes in domestic law that were necessary in order to comply with obligations deriving from membership. From the opposition front bench, Peter Shore argued against it on economic and constitutional grounds. An economically-weak UK would have to make a substantial contribution across the balance of payments to the economies of the existing six member states. Membership would tie the hands of parliament, clause 2 of the bill not only committing the country to existing EC law but to future EC law as well: it would become law without the assent of parliament.

Over the course of the three days, no Labour MP rose to support the bill. Some expressed support for the concept of the EEC but not for the provisions of the bill. Four Conservatives spoke against it, largely on the constitutional grounds outlined by Shore. The four included the Conservative MP for Wolverhampton South-West, Enoch Powell. Parliament, he argued, would lose its legislative supremacy and the house of commons would lose its exclusive control over taxation and expenditure. The debate was wound up by the prime minister. He reiterated the case for membership and made clear that if the vote was lost: 'this Parliament cannot sensibly continue'.[20]

The second reading was carried by 309 votes to 301, a government majority of eight.[21] Despite being made a vote of confidence, 15 Conservatives voted against it and a further five abstained from voting. On the Labour side, five members abstained.[22] Without the Labour abstentions and the votes of five Liberal MPs, the bill would have been lost. As *The Times* recorded the following morning: 'The Government came within a hair's breadth of falling in the Commons last night. After they had carried the second reading of the crucial European Communities Bill by a majority of only eight votes Mr Heath, pale and tense, took up a challenge from Mr Wilson and said the Government would fight on. But every politician in the crowded Commons who heard him knew that he and the Government had suffered a severe setback that stopped short only of defeat.'[23]

For the government, the difference between a setback and a defeat was a crucial one. They had overcome the biggest hurdle in getting the bill through, albeit it with immense difficulty. A protracted committee stage lay ahead. Because it was demonstrably a bill of major constitutional significance, committee stage was taken on the floor of the House. It took five months, and throughout that period a number of committed anti-EEC Conservative MPs maintained their opposition. It was, as government chief whip, Francis Pym, observed, the most prolonged struggle of its kind.[24]

However, despite the opposition of Labour MPs and Conservative anti-marketeers, the government maintained its majority throughout the proceedings. Prior to committee stage, it carried the ways and means resolution for the bill and the money resolution, in each case by a majority of 30 votes.[25] The main dissent in each was through abstention

[20] Hansard, *Commons Debates*, 5th ser., dcccxxxi, col. 752: 17 Feb. 1972.

[21] Hansard, *Commons Debates*, 5th ser., dcccxxxi, cols 753–8: 17 Feb. 1972.

[22] Norton, *Dissension in the House of Commons 1945–74*, pp. 405–6.

[23] *The Times*, 18 Feb. 1972.

[24] Norton, *Conservative Dissidents*, 75.

[25] Norton, *Dissension in the House of Commons 1945–74*, pp. 406–8.

rather than by vote; only three Conservatives voted against the government in the first vote and two in the second. On 1 March, the government successfully resisted an opposition motion challenging the ruling of the chairman of ways and means that the bill was not a bill to approve the treaty of accession but a bill to give effect to the 'legal nuts and bolts' necessary for entry. The ruling was important in that a consequence was to limit the amendments that could be tabled and debated. The motion was defeated by 309 votes to 274, with only one Conservative MP (Powell) voting with the opposition. On 6 March, an opposition motion censuring the restricted drafting of the bill was defeated by a majority of 47 votes, no Conservatives cross voting and only three abstaining; five Labour MPs abstained.

Committee stage began on 1 March. Conservative MPs voted with the opposition on 18 substantive amendments to clause 1 (short title and interpretation) as well as on the motion that the clause stand part of the bill. However, the number of tory MPs cross voting was not sufficient to rob the government of its majority. It achieved majorities ranging from eight to 49. The number of Conservatives cross voting ranged from one to 22. However, the division that maximised Conservative opposition was also the one that maximised dissension on the Labour benches. Conservative MP, Neil Marten, moved an amendment to provide for a consultative advisory referendum before the act came into force. It was rejected by 284 votes to 235, a government majority of 49. Although 22 Conservatives voted for the amendment, 63 Labour MPs abstained from voting, as did nine Conservatives. The issue had badly split the Labour Party, the deputy leader, Roy Jenkins, having resigned, along with Harold Lever and George Thompson, from the shadow cabinet, on the issue.[26] On 19 April, the motion that clause 1 stand part of the bill was put and carried by 152 votes to 135.

Clause 2, on the general implementation of the treaties, gave the force of law in the UK to rights, powers, liabilities, obligations and restrictions from time to time created or arising under the treaties. It was a particular target of opposition from Conservatives who regarded it as an attack on parliamentary sovereignty. Conservative anti-marketeers voted with the opposition on 23 substantive amendments as well as on the motion that the clause stand part of the bill. At one point the government's majority fell to four. The government had another success in being able to carry a guillotine motion, limiting the remaining days in committee to 12. That, as the leader of the House, Robert Carr, pointed out, would mean that on completion, the committee stage had occupied 26 days. The motion was carried by 304 votes to 293. Fifteen Conservatives voted against and a further eight abstained from voting (as did four Labour members). On 14 June, the motion that clause 2 stand part of the bill was carried by 296 votes to 288, a majority of eight. There had been fears that the government might lose the vote, but in the event there was a virtual rerun of the situation on second reading. Fifteen Conservatives voted against the clause, and a further eight abstained from voting, but the government was saved by the votes of five Liberals and by the abstention of nine Labour members. 'It was', as *The Times* noted, 'an agonisingly close call for the Government.'[27]

---

[26] Roy Jenkins, *A Life at the Centre* (1991), 341–9; Kitzinger, *Diplomacy and Persuasion*, 390–5; Owen, *Time to Declare*, 191–202.

[27] *The Times*, 15 June 1972.

Conservative opponents of the bill continued to vote with the opposition on remaining clauses and the schedules to the bill.[28] Typically, 11 or 12 Conservatives would vote in the opposition lobby – on some occasions, mustering 14 members – but not enough to threaten the government's majority. On one occasion, on an amendment to clause 8, the government's majority fell to eight, but there was not the same uncertainty over the outcome as there had been on second reading and on the division on clause 2.

Committee stage concluded on 5 July. Despite the sustained opposition from Labour MPs and dissident Conservatives, the government had avoided losing a vote. This had a major, and intended, procedural advantage. If committee stage of a bill is taken on the floor of the House and is not amended, there is no report stage. The bill thus proceeded straight to third reading. Taken on 13 July, third reading was carried by 301 votes to 284, a government majority of 17. Sixteen Conservatives voted against and four abstained from voting. Thirteen Labour MPs also abstained. The relief on the government benches was reflected in the actions of the government chief whip, Francis Pym. 'Much to the delight and amusement of us all', recorded cabinet minister, Jim Prior, 'this cautious and phlegmatic character danced a jig on the floor of the House.'[29]

The bill had witnessed sustained opposition from a number of Conservative MPs. Eighty-five votes (out of 104) witnessed one or more Conservatives voting with the opposition. The leading opponent on the Conservative benches was Enoch Powell, who voted against the government in 80 votes, followed by John Biffen, who voted against in 78. Neil Marten voted against on 69 occasions. A further 13 Conservatives voted against in ten or more divisions.[30] It was the most sustained intra-party dissension in post-war history.

The bill had also badly split the Labour Party. Supporters of European integration had voted against the bill, against their better judgment. 'As it was', recorded David Owen, 'we humiliated ourselves night after night voting against what we believed in.'[31] However, supporters maintained contact with the government whips and sought to ensure that sufficient Labour members were absent when it looked as if the government might lose.[32] This helped ensure the passage of the bill but exacerbated tensions within Labour's ranks.

The bill then passed the house of lords with little difficulty. The preceding October, the House had voted in support of the principle of entry by 451 votes to 58. The bill spent nine days in committee but – despite 97 amendments having been tabled – it followed the Commons in being passed without amendment. Third reading was in large part taken up with the government denying that ministers were under instructions to resist all amendments. The bill was given a third reading on 20 September by 161 votes to 21.[33] It received royal assent on 17 October.

[28] Norton, *Conservative Dissidents*, 78–9.

[29] J. Prior, *A Balance of Power* (1986), 86.

[30] Norton, *Conservative Dissidents*, 80.

[31] Owen, *Time to Declare*, 187.

[32] Heath, *The Course of My Life*, 384–5.

[33] Hansard, *Lords Debates*, 5th ser., cccxxxv, cols 1272–3: 20 Sept. 1972.

2. *Consequences*

The most obvious consequence of the passage of the act was the intended one. It provided the basis in domestic law for the UK to become a member of the EC. The UK became a member of the community on 1 January 1973. It was both a specific event and the start of a process. Various new treaties and treaty amendments have been agreed since. In the UK, the changes in UK law necessary to give effect to the new treaties have been made under amending acts.[34]

Though the steps taken to provide for UK membership of the EC were constitutionally correct, they were also politically contested. Though there was no constitutional requirement for a referendum, opponents of the bill argued that such a major constitutional change should have been approved in a popular referendum. The 1970 Conservative manifesto was not regarded as a sufficient mandate, given that it provided the basis for negotiation rather than an endorsement of membership. The Labour Party, albeit for the purposes of resolving internal party differences, committed itself to renegotiation *and* a referendum.

Following the return of a Labour government in 1974, negotiations were held and changes to Britain's membership agreed.[35] None required a change to the treaties. Though not unimportant, the renegotiation was sometimes referred to in Brussels as 'the so-called renegotiation'.[36] The government's decision to hold a referendum was approved in the Commons on 9 April 1975 by 396 votes to 170. (The Lords approved by 261 to 20.) A Referendum Bill was quickly enacted and a referendum held on 5 June. The ballot paper stated that the government had announced the results of the renegotiation of the United Kingdom's terms of membership of the EC: 'Do you think that the United Kingdom should stay in the European Community (the Common Market)?' The doctrine of collective ministerial responsibility was suspended so that ministers could argue on different sides in the campaign. Following the campaign, in which the 'yes' side massively out-spent the other side, the result was 17,378,581 votes for 'yes' and 8,470,073 votes for 'no'. The turnout was estimated at 65%. The vote was seen as settling the issue of British membership of the EC. In practice, it did no such thing – membership continued as a politically-contested issue – but was, arguably, more important constitutionally in setting a precedent for UK-wide referendums.

Membership of the EC – now the European Union – has had profound economic and political consequences, though whether those consequences have been beneficial or harmful has been a matter of debate. There are those who continue to press for greater European integration and bodies, such as the Bruges group, that are sceptical of membership – and parties, most notably the United Kingdom Independence Party (UKIP), which favour withdrawal from membership. However, in constitutional terms, membership has had a major impact on the role of, and the relationship between, the courts and of parliament.

The novel constitutional situation created by membership was summarized in the government white paper in 1967 on the legal and constitutional position of membership:

[34] European Communities (Amendment) Act 1986, 1993, 1998, 2001, 2002; European Union (Accessions) Act 2003; European Union (Amendment) Act 2008.

[35] See Harold Wilson, *The Final Term: The Labour Government 1974–1976* (1979), 83–109.

[36] David Butler and Uwe Kitzinger, *The 1975 Referendum* (1976), 39.

The constitutional innovation would lie in the acceptance in advance as part of the law of the United Kingdom of provisions to be made in the future by instruments issued by the Community institutions – a situation for which there is no precedent in this country. However, these instruments, like ordinary delegated legislation, would derive their force under the law of the United Kingdom from the original enactment passed by Parliament.[37]

In short, law emanating from the EC would have effect in the UK without parliament having to give its assent. That assent would, in effect, have been given in advance under the provisions of the 1972 act. The doctrine of parliamentary sovereignty remained extant in that parliament could repeal the act. However, so long as the 1972 act remains in force, parliament is constrained, albeit by its own actions. It could affect the implementation of EC directives but had no say over regulations, which had direct effect.

Case law of the European Court of Justice (ECJ) also meant that EC law was to take priority over UK law if the two came into conflict. Section 2 of the 1972 act provided that UK law should be construed in order to comply with EC law and directly applicable provisions should prevail over UK acts in so far as they were inconsistent with them. This created a new role for the courts. Whereas the courts previously had the power of statutory interpretation, discerning the intent of parliament, now they were in a position where, in the event of a conflict between EC and UK law, they could hold that a provision of UK law was incompatible with EC law. The novel situation was one that the courts had difficulty in adjusting to, the master of the rolls, Lord Denning, asserting in 1976 that when acts were passed by parliament the courts would abide by them without regard to the EC treaty, but three years later declaring that if UK law was inconsistent with EC law: 'then it is our bounden duty to give priority to Community law'.[38]

The most celebrated case, or series of cases, in which the supremacy of EC law was asserted was the *Factortame* cases in 1990–1 relating to the Merchant Shipping Act 1988. Following an opinion of the ECJ, the house of lords held that a measure of UK law could be suspended where it appeared in conflict with EC law until a final determination was made and later that compensatory damages could be awarded where a provision of a law passed by parliament violated a provision of the EC treaty.[39] (Accepting that an interlocutory injunction against the crown could be granted has since been extended by the courts outside the context of EC law.)[40] In 1994, in *R v. Secretary of State for Employment ex p Equal Opportunities Commission*,[41] the house of lords declared certain provisions of the 1978 Employment Protection (Consolidation) Act unlawful as they were incompatible with EC law. *The Times* declared the following day that: 'Britain may now have, for the first time in its history a constitutional court'.[42] As Patricia Maxwell observed:

---

[37] Lord Chancellor's Department, *Legal and Constitutional Implications of United Kingdom Membership of the European Communities*, Cmnd. 3301 (1967).

[38] Quoted in A.W. Bradley and K.D. Ewing, *Constitutional and Administrative Law* (14th edn, 2007), 144.

[39] F.G. Jacobs, 'Public Law: The Impact of Europe', *Public Law* (1999), 241–5; Bradley and Ewing, *Constitutional and Administrative Law*, 133–5, 145–7.

[40] Jacobs, 'Public Law: The Impact of Europe', 242.

[41] *R v. Secretary of State for Employment ex p Equal Opportunities Commission* [1994] 2 WLR 409.

[42] *The Times*, 5 Mar. 1994.

The Lords have abandoned the fiction that the courts are concerned only to ascertain and implement the intentions of Parliament. The fact that they did not even pay lip service to the assumed limitations of their office perhaps inevitably produced disquiet of the kind expressed in *The Times.* The case demonstrates the increasing willingness of the judiciary to review executive decision-making once believed to be outside the courts' control, not least in the European arena.[43]

The constitutional lawyer, Sir William Wade, described the courts as having implemented in *Factortame*[44] a 'constitutional revolution', but as Patrick Birkinshaw has observed: 'it was a revolution that should have been foreseen'.[45] During passage of the bill in 1972, ministers asserted that it would not affect parliamentary sovereignty – Sir Geoffrey Howe asserting that 'the ultimate supremacy of Parliament will not be affected, and it will not be affected because it cannot be affected'[46] – but this was correct only inasmuch as parliament enacted the 1972 act and could repeal the 1972 act. So long as it was on the statute book, the outputs of parliament could be set aside by a body other than parliament.

The effect of the 1972 act was not only to limit parliament in what it could enact but also imposed a notable and unexpected burden. The act made provision for subordinate legislation to be introduced to give effect to community obligations. Though certain subjects could not be subject to such subordinate legislation, such as an increase in taxation, the scope was broad. As Bradley and Ewing note, the government did not expect the power to be frequently used, 'an expectation which was clearly unfulfilled'.[47] If parliament was to have a role in scrutinising such legislation, it needed a specific procedure for so doing.

Though parliament was not part of the EC law-making process – as we have seen, it had already given assent to measures under the terms of the 1972 act – it could at least seek to scrutinise proposals being submitted to the council of ministers and influence ministers before they attended the council. No specific provision for such scrutiny was provided for at the time of the passage of the bill in 1972, though the government accepted the need for special arrangements to consider draft regulations and directives. It, therefore, proposed the creation of *ad hoc* committees in the two Houses to make proposals for such scrutiny. As a result of the recommendations of these committees (the Foster committee in the Commons and the Maybray-King committee in the Lords), the two Houses established dedicated means of scrutiny for EC legislation.[48]

Each year, the government submits approximately 1,000 EU documents to parliament (the relevant department also supplying now an explanatory memorandum for each document) and these are considered by the EU scrutiny committee (originally the select

[43] Patricia Maxwell, 'The House of Lords as a Constitutional Court: The Implications of *Ex Parte EOC*', in *The House of Lords: Its Parliamentary and Judicial Roles*, ed. Paul Carmichael and Bruce Dickson (Oxford, 1999), 210.

[44] *Factortame* v. *Secretary of State for Transport (No 2)* [1991] 1 All ER 70 (ECJ and HL).

[45] Patrick Birkinshaw, *European Public Law* (2003), 193.

[46] Hansard, *Commons Debates*, 5th ser., dcccxl, col. 627: 5 July 1972; see also Norton, *Dissension in the House of Commons 1945–74*, pp. 491–2.

[47] Bradley and Ewing, *Constitutional and Administrative Law*, 141.

[48] See Philip Norton, 'The United Kingdom: Political Conflict, Parliamentary Scrutiny', in *National Parliaments and the European Union*, ed. Philip Norton (1996), 92–109.

committee on European legislation) in the Commons and the European Union committee (originally the European Communities committee) in the Lords. The EU scrutiny committee is the best resourced of Commons' select committees; it considers each document for its legal and political significance and publishes a weekly report. Where it considers a document is of such political or legal significance as to merit further consideration, it can recommend it be considered for debate in a European committee or on the floor of the House. Where a document is referred to a European committee (a 13-member committee nominated for the purpose), the relevant minister can be questioned for an hour, followed by a 90-minute debate. Debates on the floor of the House are rare.

The Lords does not consider every document but, instead, undertakes an initial sift and sends documents that raise significant issues to one of seven subcommittees. Each subcommittee covers particular policy sectors and comprises one or two members of the main committee and about ten co-opted members. The result is that over 70 members of the House are engaged on regular scrutiny of EU documents. The subcommittees examine the documents and also undertake inquiries of their own, operating the same way as select committees, calling for evidence, interviewing witnesses and publishing – generally authoritative and well-regarded – reports. The main committee also undertakes inquiries on issues affecting the EU, such as the proposal for a second chamber of the European parliament and the Lisbon treaty. If a report is recommended by the committee for debate in the House, then time is found to debate it.

The committees in the two Houses complement one another, the Commons going for breadth and the Lords for depth.[49] They benefit from the explanatory memoranda submitted by departments and also the scrutiny reserve – the commitment by government not to give assent to any measure in the council of ministers until it has cleared scrutiny in both Houses. A committee may thus hold a document 'under scrutiny' as a way of putting pressure on the government to provide more information or pay greater heed to some of the concerns it has about the document. However, there are circumstances in which the government can override the scrutiny reserve, and variously does so.[50] The reports of the committees are formally for the information of the respective House and, in practice, tend to inform debate on a subject – especially, as is sometimes the case with Lords' reports, if they get in at an early stage – but with limited evidence of them changing the outcomes of particular proposals.

The Lisbon treaty gives national parliaments, for the first time, a formal role in the EU law-making process (in referring back to the council of ministers proposals deemed to conflict with the principle of subsidiarity), though the effect is likely to be limited.[51] In practice, national parliaments remain external to the process of European law-making; their principal relationship is with their national governments rather than the institutions of the EU.

[49] Philip Norton, *Parliament in British Politics* (Basingstoke, 2005), 143.

[50] See Appendix 1 in House of Commons European Scrutiny Committee, *The Work of the Committee in 2008–09*, Sixth Report of Session 2009–10, HC 267 (2010).

[51] See House of Lords European Union Committee, *The Treaty of Lisbon: An Impact Assessment*, Tenth Report of Session 2007–08, HL Paper 62–1 (2008), 234–46. Few measures fall foul of the principle. The more relevant basis for challenge is on grounds of proportionality. National parliaments, though, are increasing their sharing of information, both formally – through the Conference of Community and European Affairs Committees of Parliaments of the European Union (known by the French acronym COSAC) – and informally.

However, each member state has a role in the law-making process through their respective ministers in the council of ministers (and through their head of government at the meetings of the European Council) and through the members they elect to the European parliament. When the UK joined the EC, membership of the European parliament (formally, at the time, the European assembly) was by appointment from membership of national parliaments and not by election. It was only as a result of treaties subsequent to UK membership in 1973 that direct election to the European parliament was introduced and also changes in the relationship between member states and the institutions were effected.

As a result of membership, the UK thus had to adapt its own constitutional arrangements as well as develop a new relationship with a supranational body. The UK acquired obligations that it was required to fulfil and for which it could be judicially challenged in the event of a failure to fulfil them. In 2009, for example, the Court of Justice delivered nine judgments concerning the failure of the UK to fulfil its obligations.[52] It also acquired the opportunity to influence the decisions of the EC through the council of ministers and, especially following the Amsterdam and Lisbon treaties, through the European parliament and the process of co-decision.

The constitutional implications of membership have been more extensive than was initially conceded during the passage of the European Communities Bill, in part because the government did not fully appreciate the implications for parliament (in practical terms, in respect of the subordinate legislation that was needed and in constitutional terms, in respect of the capacity of the courts to strike down measures of UK law, even though that was a necessary implication of membership) and in part because of the scale of changes brought about by subsequent treaties, not least the Single European Act. Constitutional ambiguities remain. There is uncertainty as to the stance of the courts in the event of parliament enacting a measure expressly overriding a provision of EU law. There is no expectation of parliament doing so, but were it to do so the constitutional position is uncertain.

The motivations for UK membership of the EC were economic and political. The constitution had to be adapted to membership, an adaptation that was far from problem-free. In constitutional terms, membership was a major step, challenging, in the eyes of some critics, the settlement of 1689. Membership created a new juridical dimension to the constitution, since complemented by two other developments covered in this volume – the Human Rights Act 1998 and devolution, not least the Scotland Act 1998. The UK has had to adapt to judicial supremacy in the sphere of EU law and doubts as to the sustainability of the doctrine of parliamentary sovereignty under the changes wrought by the European Communities Act.

---

[52] The Court of Justice, *Annual Report 2009* (Luxembourg, 2009), 92–3.

Extending the Role of the Courts:
The Human Rights Act 1998

DAVID FELDMAN

The Labour Party in the 1990s supported enactment of the European Convention on Human Rights (ECHR) rights for party-political as well as principled reasons. The Human Rights Bill sought to balance parliamentary sovereignty and effective protection of rights, relying on both legal and political remedies for victims of violations. Whilst the potentially major constitutional and legal effects of the bill, which made it highly controversial from the start in the press, were partly hidden by highly-technical drafting, members of both Houses were fully aware of the scale of the bill's implications. Scrutiny was particularly rigorous in relation to the effect of decisions of the European Commission and Court of Human Rights in Strasbourg on domestic courts especially in the light of the Strasbourg organs' view of the ECHR as an evolving instrument, the position of particular interest groups such as journalistic and religious organisations, domestic courts' new obligation to interpret legislation so far as possible compatibly with the rights and their power to make a declaration of incompatibility should that prove impossible, and parliamentary scrutiny of legislation to remedy incompatibilities. Some worries have proved well founded, and political controversy has not diminished since 1998, partly because of heightened concern with measures to combat terrorism since 2001.

Keywords: capital punishment; courts; declaration of incompatibility; human rights; legislation; parliamentary sovereignty; parliament; press; public authorities; statutory interpretation

1. Origins of the Legislation

In 1950, Clement Attlee's Labour government signed, and in 1951 ratified, the European Convention for the Protection of Human Rights and Fundamental Freedoms (ECHR), albeit without great enthusiasm on the part of a majority of the cabinet,[1] who feared that it might prevent them from implementing a socialist economic programme. Some leading Conservatives were also sceptical for different reasons, doubting that any UK law could be inconsistent with the ECHR and seeing it as a potential threat to parliamentary sovereignty. All these concerns affected parts of the civil service.[2] There was, therefore, no move to give effect to convention rights in domestic law, and the UK did not accept the

---

[1] A.W.B. Simpson, *Human Rights and the End of Empire: Britain and the Genesis of the European Convention* (Oxford, 2001), ch. 14.

[2] Simpson, *Human Rights and the End of Empire*, chs 7–16; Geoffrey Marston, 'The United Kingdom's Part in the Preparation of the European Convention on Human Rights, 1950', *International and Comparative Law Quarterly*, xlii (1993), 796–826; Elizabeth Wicks, 'The United Kingdom Government's Perceptions of the European Convention on Human Rights at the Time of Entry', *Public Law* (2000), 438–55.

(originally optional) right of individuals to petition the European Commission and Court of Human Rights in respect of alleged violations by the UK. Nevertheless, some individuals in all parties saw a need to extend legal or constitutional protection for rights.[3] When Gerald Gardiner became lord chancellor in Harold Wilson's Labour government in 1964, he put his weight behind acceptance of the right of individual petition, which took effect in January 1966.[4] Once cases started to trickle to the court it gradually became clear that aspects of domestic law and practice could violate the ECHR, and successive governments consistently acted on final judgments made against the UK. But as the Labour Party moved further to the left and the Conservative Party moved to the right in the 1970s and 1980s, human rights fell out of favour with powerful elements in both parties.

Nevertheless, a growing number of people favoured introducing to domestic law at least those rights which people could already enforce in Strasbourg. Some went further, arguing for a distinctively British bill of rights, reflecting British values including commitment to the rule of law. In this latter group were some Conservative politicians, who were particularly keen to assert rights as limits to the powers of Labour governments. A number of Conservative and Liberal (later Liberal Democrat) parliamentarians introduced bills, none of which was enacted, to make fundamental rights part of domestic law as a partial antidote to the weakness of parliamentary accountability.[5]

At the 1992 general election, when John Major's Conservative government unexpectedly won a further term, only the Liberal Democrats' manifesto included a commitment to make human rights enforceable in domestic law. However, the Labour leadership under Neil Kinnock had already started to move its party back towards the political centre-ground to make it electable. A mixture of principled liberalism and political prudence made the aims of human-rights campaigners coincide with the interest of the Labour Party in reassuring electors that it was no longer committed to state control of the economy, wholesale nationalisation, and redistribution of wealth. The Labour Party's election manifesto in 1992 had, therefore, included a commitment to a non-binding charter of rights and a bill of rights which would be given effect through parliament rather than the courts.[6] Under John Smith's leadership in 1993, the party formally committed itself to incorporating the ECHR in domestic law. Tony Blair, who had previously opposed incorporation, as shadow home secretary followed the Smith line and, with Derry Irvine, his former pupil-master and future lord chancellor, laid the policy foundation to give effect to it.[7] After Mr Smith's premature death, Tony Blair, as leader, allowed the process to continue.

---

[3] See, e.g., *Liberty in the Modern State: Eight Oxford Lectures*, ed. Conservative Political Centre (1957), particularly the introduction by Peter Goldman at 7–10; but later support from Conservatives when in opposition (see, e.g., Sir Keith Joseph, *Freedom under Law* (1975), and Lord Hailsham's articles in *The Times*, 2, 16, 19 and 20 May 1975) rather than when in government.

[4] Simpson, *Human Rights and the End of Empire*, ch. 20; Anthony Lester, 'UK Acceptance of the Strasbourg Jurisdiction: What Really went on in Whitehall in 1965', *Public Law* (1998), 237–53.

[5] Conservatives who proposed, or supported, bills included Sir Edward Gardner QC, MP and Sir Geoffrey Rippon MP. Liberal supporters of the campaign included Lord Wade, Lord Lester of Herne Hill QC, Alan Beith MP and Lord Goodhart. For an account of the bills introduced to parliament between 1968 and 1997, see Michael Zander, *A Bill of Rights?* (4th edn, 1997), ch. 1.

[6] This was influenced by David Kinley, *The European Convention on Human Rights: Compliance without Incorporation* (Aldershot, 1993).

[7] See Labour Party, *A New Agenda for Democracy: Labour's Proposals for Constitutional Reform* (1993); Francesca Klug, *Values for a Godless Age: The Story of the United Kingdom's New Bill of Rights* (Harmondsworth, 2000), ch. 6.

In December 1996, in preparation for the 1997 general election, a Labour Party discussion paper set out the process by which the rights under the ECHR would be brought into domestic law.[8] There would be no limitation on the legislative competence of the queen in parliament, and courts would not be entitled to hold that statutes were invalid for inconsistency with rights. Instead, public authorities would have to act compatibly with the ECHR unless required by primary legislation to act otherwise. The aim was to foster a 'culture of human rights' in government, and allow judges to grant remedies against public authorities which violated rights. Parliament would still be able to pass any legislation it liked (subject to European Union (EU) law), but all legislation would have to be interpreted compatibly with convention rights as far as possible. If that proved impossible, the higher courts would be able to make 'declarations of incompatibility' which might (but need not) lead to legislation to rectify the incompatibility. Within parliament, a new select committee would monitor the implementation of the convention rights.

This compromise between protecting rights and parliamentary sovereignty had been worked out over a significant period in discussions between leading members of the Labour Party, particularly Jack Straw, and campaigners for human rights, including Lord Lester of Herne Hill QC (Liberal Democrat), members of non-governmental organisations (NGOs) such as the British Institute of Human Rights, the National Council on Civil Liberties (which became Liberty in 1989), the Institute for Public Policy Research, JUSTICE (the British branch of the International Commission of Jurists), and the Constitution Unit at University College London. It was part of a wide-ranging effort to construct a new philosophy, which became known as 'the Third Way', for a renewed (and New) Labour, distancing it from 'old', left-wing Labour. It sought a communitarian compromise between liberalism and socialism. Emphasizing the responsibilities which went with rights, Labour politicians stressed that their Human Rights Bill would not allow the interests of undeserving individuals to trump those of society as a whole.

The Labour government which swept to power in 1997 with a substantial Commons' majority was committed to making significant changes to the constitution. Varying degrees of devolution would be offered to Scotland and Wales, and (following the Belfast agreement in 1998) to Northern Ireland. Rights under the ECHR would act as limits on the executive and legislative competences of devolved institutions and public authorities, but would not override primary legislation. Nevertheless, popular support for the Human Rights Bill was limited, and it was unpopular from the start with large sections of the population and press. As Professor Vernon Bogdanor wrote in 2004: 'If the constitutional reforms since 1997 comprise a revolution, it has been a quiet revolution, albeit a revolution whose consequences are likely to prove very profound. . . . [They] offer a spectacle unique in the democratic world, of a country transforming its uncodified constitution into a codified one, there being neither the political will nor the consensus to do more. The end-point of this piecemeal process of constitutional reform is, therefore, unclear.'[9]

---

[8] Jack Straw and Paul Boateng, *Bringing Rights Home: Labour's Plans to Incorporate the European Convention on Human Rights into UK Law* (1996), reprinted in *European Human Rights Law Review* (1997), 71–80.

[9] Vernon Bogdanor, 'Our New Constitution', *Law Quarterly Review*, cxx (2004), 242, 246. Professor Bogdanor attributes the insight contained in the second sentence to Professor Martin Loughlin.

2. *The Shape of the Bill*

The Human Rights Bill was drafted to achieve the aims set out before the election. A range of judicial and legislative remedies would be available to correct or compensate for violations of convention rights by public authorities, but the rights would not bind parliament. Legislation was to be interpreted compatibly with the rights as far as possible. Superior courts would be able to declare that primary legislation which could not be interpreted compatibly violated a convention right (a 'declaration of incompatibility'), but that would not affect the legislation's validity or effectiveness, and nobody would be under any legal obligation to legislate to remove the incompatibility. In this way, the government argued, rights would be protected ultimately through parliamentary processes, maintaining parliamentary sovereignty.

In the house of lords, peers praised the bill's concision and clarity, and the elegance of its compromise between judicial protection and parliamentary sovereignty.[10] However, some non-lawyers finding the bill intimidatingly technical, lawyers dominated much of the debate. The bill certainly lacked rhetorical punch and was somewhat legalistic. For example, the opening clause was concerned with the 'convention rights', which it defined purely by referring to the numbers of the articles of the ECHR which contained rights that were to take effect in domestic law. The text of the rights was relegated to a schedule. Clause 2 concerned the interpretation of convention rights. The most significant provision was held back until clause 6(1), obliging public authorities to comply with convention rights unless primary legislation made that impossible. Nothing in the bill displayed the grand style usually associated with bills of rights. It was silent as to its purposes and underlying values; there was no grand statement of principle in the long title, no preamble, and no purpose clause.

The absence of anything of this sort from the bill is unlikely to have been accidental. Statutes of constitutional significance have sometimes been given explanatory preambles and expressed in imposing language.[11] One may compare the Scotland Bill, which was before parliament at the same time, and opens boldly: 'There shall be a Scottish Parliament', overturning nearly 300 years of constitutional history in a single, dramatic sentence.[12] As we shall see, the government resisted pressure to set out the grand plan in

[10] Lord Lester hyperbolically remarked: 'The Bill is brilliantly conceived and exquisitely well executed. I congratulate the Government and especially their unnamed advisers on having produced a measure of this quality' (third reading: Hansard, *Lords Debates*, 5th ser., dlxxxv, cols 834–5: 5 Feb. 1998). Earl Russell, another Liberal Democrat, said: 'The drafting of the Bill appears to me to be a thing of intellectual beauty. I admire it deeply' (second reading: Hansard, *Lords Debates*, 5th ser., dlxxxii, col. 1286: 3 Nov. 1997).

[11] The Parliament Act 1911 begins with a preamble setting out, in three short paragraphs, the purpose of the act and the Liberal government's plans for future reform of the house of lords. Five preambular paragraphs at the beginning of the Statute of Westminster 1931 outlined the reasons for, and purposes of, that act. As Lord Rodger has noted in his address as president of the Holdsworth Club, *The Form and Language of Legislation* (Birmingham, 1998), 7, the John F. Kennedy Memorial Act 1964 has three preambular paragraphs, and His Majesty's Declaration of Abdication Act 1936 begins with two preambular paragraphs which 'are a testimony to the solemn, irrevocable and far-reaching nature of the step to which Parliament was giving effect'.

[12] Lord Rodger of Earlsferry pointed out the rhetorical significance of this in *The Form and Language of Legislation*, 6: 'That is an opening worthy of any great stylist, designed for maximum effect.' If the clauses had been reordered, making clause 1 a definition clause to aid comprehension: 'From a legal point of view, it would have made no difference. From a political point of view, however, the effect would have been wholly different. And for the Secretary of State at that stage the politics of the Bill, quite properly, be at least as important as, if not more important than, the convenience of those who will one day have to interpret it.'

the bill. Why did they reject it? One may speculate that criticism had persuaded them to play down, as far as possible, the idea that the bill represented a major development of constitutional principle or relationships. But both its supporters and its critics were aware of its symbolic, political and practical importance. The lord chancellor described the bill as occupying 'a central position in our programme of constitutional reform'.[13] In recognition of the bill's constitutional importance, the committee stage in each House was taken on the floor of the House. That it was a significant bill was never in doubt; the question concerned the precise nature of its significance.

3. *The Bill in Parliament*

The bill was introduced to the house of lords on 23 October 1997, alongside the publication of a white paper.[14] Starting in the Lords allowed the government to take advantage of the Salisbury convention in the bill's early stages: the Conservative opposition in the Lords made it clear that they did not support the central aim of the bill (Lord Beloff called it 'silly, unnecessary and dangerous'),[15] but considered themselves bound not to vote against it on second reading as it had been included in the government's election manifesto.[16] Liberal Democrat peers were strongly supportive; Lord Lester of Herne Hill's frequent contributions were particularly influential.[17] In the Commons, where the Salisbury convention does not operate, the opposition divided the House on second reading, and the Conservative front bench strongly opposed changing the balance between parliament and courts, allowing judges to develop broad and indeterminate principles, using the ECHR as a basis for domestic rights, and remedial orders. Even there, the large Labour majority and a measure of support for the bill on Conservative benches were disincentives to serious attempts at wrecking.

The debate in both Houses was generally courteous and constructive, with few moments of irritation even when discussion continued late into the night (despite occasional friction over whether opposition amendments were genuinely 'probing' or were wrecking amendments in disguise).[18] The main controversies were of three kinds.

First, members wanted to make the bill as clear in its principles, scope and impact as possible. Contentious issues included the effect on parliamentary sovereignty, the nature

[13] Third reading: Hansard, *Lords Debates*, 5th ser., dlxxxv, col. 839: 5 Feb. 1998.

[14] Home Office, *Rights Brought Home: The Human Rights Bill*, Cm. 3782 (1997). For a helpful selection of extracts from the parliamentary debates, arranged thematically, see *Legislating for Human Rights: The Parliamentary Debates on the Human Rights Bill*, ed. Jonathan Cooper and Adrian Marshall-Williams (Oxford, 2000).

[15] Second reading: Hansard, *Lords Debates*, 5th ser., dlxxxii, col. 1269: 3 Nov. 1997. Lord Beloff, an eminent historian, was originally a Liberal peer but had crossed the floor to sit on the Conservative back benches.

[16] See the exchange between Lord Williams of Mostyn (under secretary of state, home office) and Lord Henley (Conservative), second reading: Hansard, *Lords Debates*, 5th ser., dlxxxii, col. 1306: 3 Nov. 1997.

[17] On third reading, Lord Ackner (a retired law lord) said: 'My Lords, my abiding recollection of this Bill will be attending the supervisions so ably administered by the noble Lord, Lord Lester, to the great satisfaction of us all. I particularly enjoyed them since I did not have to produce an essay indicating how I followed every word the noble Lord said' (Hansard, *Lords Debates*, 5th ser., dlxxxv, col. 837: 5 Feb. 1998).

[18] See, e.g., the exchange during the committee stage: Hansard, *Lords Debates*, 5th ser., dlxxxiii, col. 557: 18 Nov. 1997; that between Baroness Young and Lord Goodhart at the report stage: Hansard, *Lords Debates*, 5th ser., dlxxxiv, cols 1347–8: 19 Jan. 1998; and that between the parties' business managers: Hansard, *Lords Debates*, 5th ser., dlxxxiv, cols 1351–2: 19 Jan. 1998.

of convention rights and whether or not they were being 'incorporated', the meaning of 'public authority', and the extent to which 'remedial orders' (statutory instruments amending legislation to remove incompatibilities between legislation and convention rights) should be subject to parliamentary scrutiny.

Second, representatives of religious organisations campaigned to protect their right to uphold religious doctrines against potentially competing convention rights.

Third, Lord Wakeham as chairman of the Press Complaints Commission (PCC) campaigned against any possibility of the press becoming legally liable for interfering with people's privacy on account of the right to respect for private life under Article 8 of the ECHR.

Whilst central planks in the bill withstood challenges, there were significant amendments to the arrangements for making remedial orders, protecting religious organisations, and protecting the press.

3.1. *The Purposes of the Bill, Convention Rights and Incorporation*

'Convention rights' were defined as 'the rights and fundamental freedoms set out in – (a) Articles 2 to 12 and 14 of the Convention, and (b) Articles 1 to 3 of the First Protocol, as read with Articles 16 to 18 of the Convention.'[19] 'The convention' meant the ECHR 'as it has effect for the time being in relation to the United Kingdom'.[20] Articles 1 and 13 of the ECHR were excluded from the list of rights,[21] and protocols nos 4, 6 and 7 to the convention were excluded because they did not apply to the UK.[22] Convention rights in the list would be subject to any designated reservation to, and derogation from, them.

Some peers thought that the purpose of the bill and legal status of the rights should be clarified. Lord Simon of Glaisdale suggested amending the long title, which spoke of 'An Act to give further effect to rights and freedoms guaranteed' under the ECHR, to read: 'An Act to give domestic effect . . . '.[23] The lord chancellor considered that 'further effect' was more accurate, since convention rights could already have some effect in

---

[19] Human Rights Bill, clause 1(1).

[20] Human Rights Bill, clause 21(1).

[21] Article 1 requires states to secure the rights to everyone within their jurisdictions. Article 13 guarantees a right to an effective remedy before a national authority for any violation of a convention right. The government took the view that it was unnecessary to include them, because they merely set out what it was the purpose of the bill as a whole to achieve: Lord Williams of Mostyn, second reading: Hansard, *Lords Debates*, 5th ser., dlxxxii, col. 1308: 3 Nov. 1997; Lord Irvine of Lairg LC, committee stage: Hansard, *Lords Debates*, 5th ser., dlxxxiii, col. 475: 18 Nov. 1997; Rt. Hon. Jack Straw MP, committee stage: Hansard, *Commons Debates*, 6th ser., cccxii, cols 979–80: 20 May 1998.

[22] Protocol no. 4 prohibits imprisonment for debt (Article 1), guarantees the right to freedom of movement within the territory of the state (Article 2), and prohibits the expulsion of nationals from, and deprivation of their right to enter, the state (Article 3) and collective expulsion of aliens (Article 4). Protocol no. 6 prohibited the death penalty save in time of war. Protocol no. 7 provides for procedural safeguards for aliens who are threatened with expulsion (Article 1), guarantees a right of appeal against conviction in most criminal cases (Article 2), gives a right to compensation for wrongful conviction (Article 3), prohibits a retrial or further punishment for a criminal offence after conviction or acquittal in most cases (*ne bis in idem*: Article 4), and guarantees equality between spouses in private law (Article 5).

[23] Report stage: Hansard, *Lords Debates*, 5th ser., dlxxxv, cols 419–21: 29 Jan. 1998.

domestic law, for example, as an aid to interpreting ambiguous legislation. He thought that the purpose of the bill was clear, although he did nothing to remove uncertainty when he said: 'The purpose of the Bill is obvious: it is to enable Convention rights to be asserted directly in our domestic courts.'[24]

Did this amount to incorporation of the rights? Lord Lester drew attention to the white paper, which had spoken of 'incorporating' the rights into domestic law.[25] But Lord Irvine pointed out that primary legislation which could not be interpreted compatibly with a convention right would, nevertheless, remain effective,[26] and that it was not intended that convention rights should be directly enforceable in litigation between wholly private parties.[27] There would be a 'special relationship' between the ECHR and domestic law, but it would 'not make the Convention directly justiciable as it would if it were expressly made part of our law'.[28] The difference might appear merely semantic, but as we shall see in section 4 the view of convention rights as essentially international rather than domestic has affected legal impact.[29]

Several peers proposed including a purpose clause. The first amendment, moved by Lord Lester, would have inserted: 'The main purposes of this Act are to secure in law the Convention rights to everyone within the jurisdiction of the United Kingdom and to provide effective remedies for violation of the Convention rights within that jurisdiction.'[30] Amendment No. 2, moved by Lord Mishcon, would have inserted: 'The main purpose of this Act is to provide effective remedies for violation of the Convention rights within the jurisdiction of the United Kingdom.'[31] Either would have helped to remove uncertainty caused by the omission of the ECHR Articles 1 (whereby states undertake to secure convention rights to everyone within their jurisdictions) and 13 (providing a right to an effective remedy before a national authority for violation of a convention right), but the government stood firm against them and neither was pressed to a division.

A number of peers argued for other rights to be included. The government had decided that it could ratify protocol no. 7, once it had amended domestic law to remove inconsistencies (for example, in relation to spouses' property rights), but until then would not include it in the bill.[32] They would not ratify protocol no. 4 because that might allow many British citizens who had no right of abode to enter and remain in the UK.[33] But

---

[24] Report stage: Hansard, *Lords Debates*, 5th ser., dlxxxv, col. 1261: 29 Jan. 1998.

[25] Report stage: Hansard, *Lords Debates*, 5th ser., dlxxxiv, col. 1257: 19 Jan. 1998.

[26] Report stage: Hansard, *Lords Debates*, 5th ser., dlxxxv, cols 421–2: 29 Jan. 1998.

[27] During the third reading debate in the house of lords, Lord Irvine stressed the extensive impact that the convention rights would have on domestic law, but continued: 'What the Bill does not do is make the Convention rights themselves directly a part of our domestic law in the way that, for example, the civil wrongs of negligence, trespass or libel are part of our domestic law. Claims in those areas are all actionable in tort in cases between private individuals. But . . . we have not provided for the Convention rights to be directly justiciable in actions between private individuals' (Hansard, *Lords Debates*, 5th ser., dlxxxiv, col. 839: 5 Feb. 1998).

[28] Hansard, *Lords Debates*, 5th ser., dlxxxiv, col. 421: 5 Feb. 1998.

[29] See section 4, below.

[30] Hansard, *Lords Debates*, 5th ser., dlxxxiii, cols 467–81: 18 Nov. 1997.

[31] Hansard, *Lords Debates*, 5th ser., dlxxxiii, cols 490–1: 18 Nov. 1997.

[32] Home Office, *Rights Brought Home*, para. 4.15. This has not yet occurred.

[33] Home Office, *Rights Brought Home*, para. 4.11; Lord Williams of Mostyn (parliamentary under secretary of state, home department), committee stage: Hansard, *Lords Debates*, 5th ser., dlxxxiii, col. 504: 18 Nov. 1997.

most controversially, they refused to ratify protocol no. 6[34] or include it in the bill, because they did not see capital punishment as a constitutional matter but rather one of conscience over which parliament should retain discretion.[35]

Lord Archer of Sandwell proposed, but withdrew, an amendment to include Articles 1 and 2 of protocol no. 6 among the convention rights in the bill. When the bill reached the Commons, Kevin McNamara MP (Labour, a dedicated member of the Parliamentary Assembly of the Council of Europe) moved a similar amendment, arguing that the United Kingdom had effectively abolished the death penalty already and there was no reason to delay ratifying the protocol.[36] Despite misgivings expressed by front benchers of all the main parties that it would effectively deprive parliament of the freedom to reintroduce the death penalty, Mr McNamara pressed his amendment to a division. The government permitted its MPs a free vote, and the amendment was carried by 294 votes to 136. The government accordingly ratified protocol no. 6 and parliament amended the Armed Forces Acts to abolish the last vestiges of the death penalty.[37] Parliament cannot now reintroduce the death penalty consistently with the UK's international obligations, illustrating the gap between the theory and reality of parliamentary sovereignty.

Turning to interpretation of the rights, clause 2 required courts and tribunals to 'take into account' relevant decisions of the Strasbourg court, the (now defunct) European Commission of Human Rights, and the committee of ministers of the Council of Europe, but did not compel them to adopt the interpretations of those institutions. This prompted three questions: What would 'take into account' signify in practice? Would it not be better to require our courts to follow Strasbourg case law, not least to put some limit on the capacity of domestic judges to interpret rights more expansively than the Strasbourg court? If one wanted to give extensive leeway to our judges, why require them to take the Strasbourg case law into account at all?

The government responded that the Strasbourg case law could not be ignored, because it governed the United Kingdom's obligations in international law to which the bill would give domestic effect. The bill was, therefore, 'bringing home the jurisprudence of the Convention rights as well as the rights themselves'. Nevertheless, courts should not be forced to follow Strasbourg case law, because the Strasbourg court had no doctrine of binding precedent, viewing the ECHR as a living instrument, growing and adapting through interpretation. Nor would it be sensible to permit, but not require, domestic courts to take account of Strasbourg case law, as that could lead to different decisions on similar facts depending on whether or not courts did so.[38] The clause stood, and has forced judges to decide when it would be appropriate not to follow Strasbourg jurisprudence.[39]

---

[34] Protocol no. 6 prohibits the death penalty except in time of war.

[35] Straw and Boateng, *Bringing Rights Home*, para. 4.13; Mike O'Brien (parliamentary under secretary of state, home department), committee stage: Hansard, *Commons Debates*, 6th ser., cccxii, col. 1004: 20 May 1998.

[36] Kevin McNamara MP moving amendment no. 111, committee stage: Hansard, *Commons Debates*, 6th ser., cccxii, cols 987–92: 20 May 1998.

[37] The United Kingdom subsequently ratified protocol no. 13, prohibiting the death penalty even in time of war, and amended the Human Rights Act 1998 (HRA 1998) to include that among the convention rights in domestic law in place of protocol no. 6.

[38] Geoff Hoon MP (parliamentary secretary, lord chancellor's department), committee stage: Hansard, *Commons Debates*, 6th ser., cccxiii, col. 4022: 3 June 1998.

[39] See below, section 4.

3.2. *Public Authorities*

Under clause 6(1), it was to be unlawful for public authorities to act in a manner incompatible with a convention right, unless the action was required by legislation which could not be interpreted compatibly with the right or invalidated. Thus the concept of 'public authority' was the key to the reach of the bill. However, it was not defined beyond including courts and tribunals, excluding parliament, and providing that a private body which exercises a public function (a 'hybrid body') would be a public authority when not exercising private functions. In the Commons, Jack Straw, the home secretary, considering it neither wise nor practicable to list all bodies to which the bill would apply, sought instead 'a statement of principle to which the courts could give effect'.[40] The rights should be:

> available in proceedings involving what might be very broadly described as 'the state' . . . [W]e wanted a realistic and modern definition of the state so as to provide correspondingly wide protection against an abuse of human rights. . . . The principle of bringing rights home suggested that liability in domestic proceedings should lie with bodies in respect of whose actions the United Kingdom Government were answerable in Strasbourg. . . . Over the years, institutions have evolved that perform functions that are effectively those of the state, in its continental sense, but are not directly under the control of the state. I happen to think that that is a good thing, but it poses some difficulties for the drafting of legislation.[41]

The bill left judges to work out, case-by-case, the range of bodies subject to convention rights. By contrast, the Freedom of Information Bill (before parliament at the same time) listed the bodies to which it was to apply. Some members of both Houses thought that it offered no clear principle to guide them. 'Probing' amendments and questions to ministers revealed that the government expected that private bodies which had assumed functions which would otherwise have had to be exercised by the state, such as the City panel on take-overs and mergers, and religious and other charitable bodies, would be subject to convention rights when exercising public functions. In the Lords, the lord chancellor had asked rhetorically what would be wrong with hospices offering medical care, faith schools, charities supporting homeless people, the National Society for the Prevention of Cruelty to Children (NSPCC), or religious organisations celebrating marriages having to respect convention rights in the course of their public functions.[42]

In the mass media, the government expected that the BBC would, and Channel 4 might, be a public authority; independent television companies would not, but their regulator, the Independent Television Commission, would. Privately-owned newspapers would not be public authorities, but the Press Complaints Commission (PCC), a private, self-regulatory body without legal power, was assumed to be, at least potentially, a public authority. Other 'hybrid' bodies were expected to include Railtrack in respect of its statutory functions as regulator of rail safety, Group 4 when operating a prison, the

---

[40] Jack Straw MP, second reading: Hansard, *Commons Debates*, 6th ser., cccvi, col. 775: 16 Feb. 1998.

[41] Jack Straw MP, committee stage: Hansard, *Commons Debates*, 6th ser., cccxiv, cols 406–7: 17 June 1998.

[42] Lord Irvine, committee stage: Hansard, *Lords Debates*, 5th ser., dlxxxiii, col. 800: 24 Nov. 1997.

General Medical Council when exercising its statutory function as a regulator and disciplinary authority for the medical profession, and perhaps the Jockey Club when regulating horse racing.[43]

However, in relation to 'hybrid' bodies the bill was drafted in terms, not of a modern understanding of the state, but rather of the nature of the function the body is exercising at the relevant moment.[44] As we shall see in section 4, judges have tended not to operate as political theorists, so the wide protection for rights for which the government hoped has not eventuated.

3.3. *The Position of Religious Groups*

In the Lords, Lord Campbell of Alloway, Lord Mackay of Drumadoon, Baroness Young and the bishop of Ripon raised the difficulties which a broad application of equality, privacy and marriage rights might present to religious groups.[45] Concerns included the possibility of legal challenge to a parochial church council which objected to the appointment of a female minister, a minister who refused on conscientious grounds to marry a homosexual couple, or a faith school which refused to employ a teacher of another faith.[46] Lord Campbell in committee and Baroness Young on report tabled amendments to exclude religious groups from the category of public authorities. However, the bishop of Ripon said that the Church of England supported the bill and disclaimed any desire to be exempt from its obligations, whilst the government made it clear that it expected churches to comply with convention rights; if there were to be a conflict between religion and a convention right, courts would have to apply the convention right and courts would prevail.[47]

Nevertheless, support for special treatment of religious groups grew, and started to derail the bill's timetable. The government sought to be conciliatory by tabling an amendment on report in the Lords to prevent ministers from making remedial orders to amend Church of England measures,[48] but this did not satisfy critics. At third reading, amendments supported by the bishops and leaders of the Church of Scotland were agreed after a division in which the government was defeated.[49] These provided a defence for a person who infringes a convention right while acting 'in pursuance of a

---

[43] Lord Irvine, committee stage: Hansard, *Lords Debates*, 5th ser., dlxxxiii, col. 800: 24 Nov. 1997, and see Jack Straw MP, committee stage: Hansard, *Commons Debates*, 6th ser., cccxii, col. 1018: 20 May 1998, and cccxiv, cols 406–13: 17 June 1998.

[44] This point was made by Sir Brian Mawhinney MP, committee stage: Hansard, *Commons Debates*, 6th ser., cccxii, cols 1031–4: 20 May 1998.

[45] See, e.g., Lord Mackay of Drumadoon, committee stage: Hansard, *Lords Debates*, 5th ser., dlxxxiii, col. 552: 18 Nov. 1997; bishop of Ripon, report stage: Hansard, *Lords Debates*, 5th ser., dlxxxiv, cols 1324–7: 19 Jan. 1998.

[46] Baroness Young, committee stage: Hansard, *Lords Debates*, 5th ser., dlxxxiii, cols 790, 800–1: 24 Nov. 1997.

[47] Report stage: Hansard, *Lords Debates*, 5th ser., dlxxxiv, cols 1320 (Baroness Young), 1325 (bishop of Ripon), 1284 (Lord Hardie, lord advocate) respectively: 19 Jan. 1998.

[48] Lord Williams of Mostyn, report stage: Hansard, *Lords Debates*, 5th ser., dlxxxv, col. 395: 29 Jan. 1998.

[49] See, e.g., Lord Campbell of Alloway, third reading: Hansard, *Lords Debates*, 5th ser., dlxxxv, cols 747–60 (amendment withdrawn): 5 Feb. 1998; Baroness Young, cols 770–3, 790–1, 812–3; bishop of Ripon, cols 773–5, 791–2; Lord Mackay of Drumadoon, cols 805, 813–7 (amendment withdrawn); for the division, see cols 788–90.

manifestation of religious belief in accordance with the historic teaching and practices of a christian or other principal religious tradition represented in Great Britain'. They also added provisions to prevent 'any minister, official or other person acting on behalf of a Christian or other principal religious tradition represented in Great Britain' from being compelled 'to administer a marriage contrary to his religious doctrines or convictions', and to ensure that educational establishments of a religious kind and religious charities remain free to select for senior positions 'people whose beliefs and manner of life are appropriate to the basic ethos of' the school or charity, and to remove from a senior post anyone 'whose beliefs and manner of life are not appropriate to' that ethos. Finally, they amended the definition of 'convention right' to make the rights subject to those provisions. This would have prevented a court making a declaration of incompatibility in respect of a Church measure, or interpreting rights in such a way as to lead to anyone being liable for violating the rights when manifesting a religious belief falling within the scope of the provisions. However, as the ECHR does not privilege any qualified right (such as the right to manifest a belief) over others, the provisions could, themselves, have violated convention rights and become the subject of a declaration of incompatibility.

The government hoped to reverse its defeat in the Commons, but on second reading it became clear that religious organisations enjoyed considerable support there, too. After discussion with the churches, the government proposed to remove the Lords' amendments with a compromise whereby a court, when determining any question arising under the act which 'might affect the exercise by – (a) a religious organisation (itself or its members collectively); or (b) a charity with a religious foundation (itself or its members collectively) of the Convention right to the freedom of thought, conscience and religion', would have to 'have particular regard to the importance of that right'.

Justifying this, the home secretary argued that the Lords' amendments protected only the principal religious traditions and would have discriminated unfairly against less-established traditions. He accepted that members of a faith organisation should sometimes be allowed to appoint staff who reflected its ethos or follow their consciences on matters concerning marriage, but he thought that the bill, as a constitutional measure, should not be overloaded with detailed matters of family, education or employment law. The government preferred to deal with those matters in the School Standards and Framework Bill which was then making its way through parliament, and in legislation on employment and families.[50]

Arguing for more concrete and extensive protection, Edward Leigh MP (Conservative) made two important points.[51] First, whilst the Strasbourg court had not yet allowed other rights to override religious freedom or restrict prayer in schools, the court might develop its jurisprudence in that direction. (Indeed, this may now be happening, as noted in section 4 below.) Second, judges in the UK might interpret convention rights more expansively than the Strasbourg court, imposing equally extensive obligations on reli-

---

[50] Jack Straw MP, committee stage: Hansard, *Commons Debates*, 6th ser., cccxii, cols 1016–29: 20 May 1998. Some safeguards in relation to staff of religious schools were encapsulated in School Standards and Framework Act 1998, sections 59 and 60. In relation to admissions, section 86(3)(b) exempts religious foundation and voluntary-aided schools from the duty to give effect to parental preference of school where complying with the preference would be incompatible with special arrangements to preserve the school's religious character.

[51] Jack Straw MP, committee stage: Hansard, *Commons Debates*, 6th ser., cccxii, cols 1046–7, 1049–50: 20 May 1998.

gious bodies. This has not so far happened, but both points illustrate the principled concern of some parliamentarians that the bill would allow domestic or international judges to reshape society in unpredictable ways. Nevertheless, the government's more limited proposal carried the day, and now forms section 13 of the act.

3.4. *The Position of the Press*

The press and their supporters feared that courts might use the right to respect for private life under Article 8 of the ECHR to give people a right to sue for invasion of privacy for the first time. Lord Wakeham, then chairman of the PCC, published an article in the *Mail on Sunday* claiming that the bill would be a villain's charter, allowing the rich, the powerful and the royal family to hide disreputable activities.[52] On second reading in the Lords, he suggested that the bill should be amended to prevent the courts becoming involved in policing the press, arguing that the system of voluntary self-regulation by the press through the PCC worked well despite its lack of legal power and the dominant presence of newspaper editors. On third reading, his claim that the bill was a threat to press self-regulation was contested by Lord Simon of Glaisdale[53] and the government successfully resisted the proposed amendment, but undertook to consider the matter further when the bill was in the Commons, where the press were well supported by former journalists, columnists, and MPs, who, for other reasons, could ill afford to alienate editors. Discussions between home office ministers and Lord Wakeham resulted in a government commitment at second reading in the Commons to draft a new clause which would virtually eliminate *ex parte* injunctions restraining publication, and would require courts to have particular regard to freedom of expression when deciding any issue which might have an impact on it and to take account of the public interest in publication and whether the publisher had complied with any relevant privacy code (such as that promulgated by the PCC).[54] When the government moved its clause at committee stage in the Commons, Lord Wakeham pronounced himself satisfied.[55] However, this did not stop others from trying to give freedom of expression priority over other rights.

The government tried to reassure MPs that newspapers and commercial television and radio stations would not be public authorities and so would not be subject to Article 8 (although the PCC would probably be a public authority on account of its public functions),[56] and argued that it would be wrong to elevate press freedom above all other rights, including the rights to life and to freedom from torture. Moreover, Strasbourg case law gave no reason to fear that Article 8 could trump Article 10.[57] In addition, Strasbourg jurisprudence allowed no such lexical ordering of qualified rights. During the debate,

[52] Lord Wakeham, *Mail on Sunday*, 2 Nov. 1997. Lord Lester described the article as 'intemperate': second reading: Hansard, *Lords Debates*, 5th ser., dlxxxii, col. 1241: 3 Nov. 1997.

[53] Third reading: Hansard, *Lords Debates*, 5th ser., dlxxxv, cols 830–3 (Lord Wakeham), 833–4 (Lord Simon): 5 Feb. 1998.

[54] Jack Straw MP, second reading: Hansard, *Commons Debates*, 6th ser., cccvi, cols 773–5: 16 Feb. 1998.

[55] See Jack Straw MP, committee stage: Hansard, *Commons Debates*, 6th ser., cccxv, col. 541: 2 July 1998.

[56] In the Lords, having initially doubted this, the lord chancellor had changed his mind: see committee stage: Hansard, *Lords Debates*, 5th ser., dlxxxiii, col. 784: 24 Nov. 1997.

[57] Jack Straw MP, committee stage: Hansard, *Commons Debates*, 6th ser., cccxv, col. 535: 2 July 1998.

MPs who complained that the protection for the press was too limited were balanced by others who stressed the need to protect ordinary or vulnerable people whose privacy was destroyed by journalists and photographers after being inadvertently caught up in newsworthy events, and doubted the capacity of the PCC to offer adequate protection.[58] Gradually a consensus developed that the government's new clause struck an appropriate balance, and, to many people's surprise, it was eventually agreed without a division.[59] As we shall see in section 4 below, it did not produce entirely the results for which the press hoped.

3.5. *Scrutiny of Remedial Orders*

In the house of lords, the select committee on delegated powers and deregulation drew the attention of the House to the provisions conferring on ministers power to make a statutory instrument (a 'remedial order') to amend or repeal legislation, including primary legislation, which had been declared by a UK court or adjudged by the Strasbourg court to be incompatible with a convention right. The committee characterised this as a 'Henry VIII' provision (giving power to a person or body other than the queen in parliament to amend or repeal an act of parliament), and recommended that there should be additional safeguards for parliamentary sovereignty, including provision for the text of a remedial order to be amended during its passage through parliament.[60] In committee, Lord Campbell of Alloway initiated a vigorous debate on this. Conservative peers argued that only primary legislation should be used to amend primary legislation.

The government and the Liberal Democrats urged that a remedial order should be a genuinely speedy way of removing legislative incompatibilities with convention rights, and pointed out that it could not harm people to make legislation rights-compliant. An amendment to remove remedial orders from the bill was defeated, but further amendments aimed to introduce parliamentary scrutiny of remedial orders and to narrow their potential width; for example, the bishops drew attention to the incongruity of amending measures of the Church of England's general synod by way of a statutory instrument.[61] As the clamour grew, both sides agreed to reflect on the debate.[62]

On report it was announced that the government had agreed to remove Church legislation from the threat of remedial orders.[63] But under continued attack, Lord Irvine finally conceded a requirement for parliamentary scrutiny of them in draft as well as in their final form, except in urgent cases.

[58] See, e.g., committee stage: Hansard, *Commons Debates*, 6th ser., cccxv, cols 547–56: 2 July 1998. At col. 555, Martin Linton MP said: 'Only 27 out of 3,023 cases before the PCC in 1996 – the last year for which figures are available – were upheld. It cannot be maintained that such regulation is a success. I have been alarmed at the reluctance with which the press, and Lord Wakeham in particular, have conceded inch by inch that press regulation is inadequate.'

[59] Committee stage: Hansard, *Commons Debates*, 6th ser., cccxv, cols 556 (Dominic Grieve MP) and 563 (agreement without division): 2 July 1998.

[60] House of Lords Select Committee on Delegated Powers and Deregulation, Sixth Report of Session 1997–98, HL Paper 32 (1997), paras 22–5.

[61] Committee stage: Hansard, *Lords Debates*, 5th ser., dlxxxiii, cols 1109–20: 27 Nov. 1997.

[62] Committee stage: Hansard, *Lords Debates*, 5th ser., dlxxxiii, col. 1151: 27 Nov. 1997.

[63] Report stage: Hansard, *Lords Debates*, 5th ser., dlxxxiv, cols 1279 (Lord Campbell of Alloway), 1346–7 (Lord Irvine): 19 Jan. 1998.

In the Commons, the opposition raised other concerns about remedial orders. As the Strasbourg court treats the ECHR as a living instrument, and might develop the rights further than was acceptable to the UK and force the UK, using a remedial order to implement Strasbourg judgments against the UK could compromise parliamentary sovereignty. Domestic courts might also extend the scope of rights beyond anything envisaged by parliament, make a declaration of incompatibility in relation to an act, and (if a consistent practice arose of legislating by remedial order in response to such declarations) trigger remedial orders in cases which the claimant might have lost had the case gone to Strasbourg. Robert Maclennan MP (Liberal Democrat) pointed out that there would be no process by which the government could challenge a declaration of incompatibility made by the highest available court in the UK, whereas a victim dissatisfied with the response to a declaration of incompatibility would be able to petition the Strasbourg court, which would be unlikely to differ from the UK's highest court. The government would then have an obligation under international law either to give effect to the judgment or derogate from the convention. As a result, the view that the bill maintained parliamentary sovereignty was a fiction. Mr Maclennan did not regret this, believing parliamentary sovereignty to be 'a doctrine at least 100 years out of date'.[64]

But most MPs supported parliamentary sovereignty.[65] Edward Garnier MP, therefore, proposed that a minister should be allowed to certify in individual cases that a declaration of incompatibility should not have effect (that is, trigger an opportunity for a remedial order) unless, and until, the case has been considered by the Strasbourg court and the British court's assessment upheld.[66] The home secretary replied that ministerial certification would serve no purpose, as the victim would probably take the case to Strasbourg anyway.[67] Dominic Grieve MP (Conservative) supported him on this, pointing out that parliament would still have the option of disregarding the Strasbourg judgment or the declaration.[68]

Mr Garnier also attacked the breadth of the remedial power and limited opportunities for parliamentary scrutiny, calling it a Henry XVI power (by implication twice as bad as a Henry VIII power) which constitutionally 'stinks'.[69] However, the home secretary saw off the challenge, saying that the previous Conservative government had introduced more far-reaching powers with less parliamentary control.[70]

[64] Committee stage: Hansard, *Commons Debates*, 6th ser., cccxiv, col. 1124: 24 June 1998; Mr Maclennan would have preferred 'a genuine separation of powers, rather than lip service being paid to it, and sovereignty to rest with the people'.

[65] See, e.g., Hansard, *Commons Debates*, 6th ser., cccxiv, cols 1124 (Edward Leigh, Conservative), 1128 (Jack Straw): 24 June 1998.

[66] Committee stage: Hansard, *Commons Debates*, 6th ser., cccxiv, cols 1116–9: 24 June 1998.

[67] Committee stage: Hansard, *Commons Debates*, 6th ser., cccxiv, cols 1122–3: 24 June 1998.

[68] Committee stage: Hansard, *Commons Debates*, 6th ser., cccxiv, cols 1126–7: 24 June 1998.

[69] Committee stage: Hansard, *Commons Debates*, 6th ser., cccxiv, col. 1136: 24 June 1998.

[70] Committee stage: Hansard, *Commons Debates*, 6th ser., cccxiv, col. 1137: 24 June 1998, referring to the Deregulation and Contracting Out Act 1994. Whilst this was true, Labour administrations later went even further than the Conservatives in the Regulatory Reform Act 2001, the Civil Contingencies Act 2004 and the Legislative and Regulatory Reform Act 2006.

Thereafter, the Commons' third reading was uneventful, the Lords accepted the Commons' amendments, and the bill received royal assent on 9 November 1998. After a period for preparation by public authorities, the act came fully into force on 2 October 2000.

4. *Impact of the Act*

This section cannot offer a full survey of the impact of the Human Rights Act (HRA), but concentrates on matters related to the main issues raised during the debates.

4.1. *Effect on Government and Public Administration*

In 2006, a review by the department for constitutional affairs concluded that judicial decisions on the act had not significantly affected the criminal law or its enforcement. They had had an effect on counter-terrorism policy, but less than had judgments of the Strasbourg court. The need to take account of convention rights had improved the quality and transparency of policy making within government, and (partly due to the work of the joint committee on human rights) accountability to parliament. However, some public authorities and members of the public had exaggerated the extent to which convention rights had caused difficulties, so the government would strengthen its guidance to clarify how the act and convention rights really worked.[71]

Many important bodies successfully promoted a culture of rights as the government had hoped.[72] For example, police training emphasized how the values underpinning convention rights – dignity, fairness, rationality in decision making, equality, pluralism, autonomy, responsibility and tolerance, among others – were consistent with the values and objectives of modern policing. However, some bodies tried, instead, to secure compliance by emphasizing the risk of legal liability rather than the congruence between human-rights principles and values of public service and good administration. This could generate defensiveness, and did not encourage humane decision making, improve practice, or engage the interest of front-line staff. It sometimes avoided a (usually tiny) risk of violating rights, but at the cost of changing professional relationships in ways which tended to undermine the values underpinning both human rights and the ethos of public service. The audit commission reported in 2003: '58 per cent of public bodies surveyed still have not adopted a strategy for human rights. In many local authorities the Act has not left the desks of the lawyers. In health, 73 per cent of trusts are not taking action. . . . In the criminal justice sector the initial flurry of activity has stopped.'

---

[71] Department for Constitutional Affairs, *Review of the Implementation of the Human Rights Act* (2006).

[72] The rights were integrated in advice given by the Treasury Solicitor, *The Judge over your Shoulder* (4th edn, 2006), available at *http://www.tsol.gov.uk/Publications/services.htm* (accessed 10 Oct. 2010), and excellent accounts of the rights and their impact are offered in Department for Constitutional Affairs, *Human Rights: Human Lives – a Handbook for Public Authorities* (2006), aimed at public authorities, and Department for Constitutional Affairs, *A Guide to the Human Rights Act 1998* (3rd edn, 2006), aimed at the general public. Both are available at *http://www.justice.gov.uk/guidance/humanrights.htm* (accessed 10 Oct. 2010).

Only 39% of public bodies were taking action to ensure that contractors were taking reasonable steps to comply with convention rights.[73] Even now, the parliamentary and health service ombudsman's guidance on good administration makes no express reference to the act or human rights.[74]

Nevertheless, the risk of legal sanctions under the act has forced decision makers to keep convention rights in the back, and sometimes at the front, of their minds. If the act has not consistently produced a culture of rights, it has, at least, advanced a culture of justification in which authorities, courts and tribunals assess decisions and actions (their own and other people's) partly by reference to convention rights.[75] This has often affected public authorities for the better.

4.2. *Effect on the Law*

Leaving aside the major impact of convention rights on the work of devolved institutions in Scotland, Wales and Northern Ireland, resulting from the devolution legislation the HRA itself has stimulated a vigorous jurisprudence concerning, among other things, several areas which caused controversy during the bill's parliamentary passage.

The status of the convention rights under the act has caused difficulty. Recognizing that they are the rights operating on the UK in international law, domestic courts generally follow the Strasbourg court, offering no less, but no more, protection than that court; contrary to some people's expectations, the HRA has not become a genuinely British bill of rights or stimulated distinctively British ways of approaching rights.[76] However, courts have departed from the Strasbourg line where they have been bound by a conflicting decision of a higher domestic court,[77] or the Strasbourg court has left the state a margin of appreciation,[78] or domestic judges think that the Strasbourg court has misunderstood domestic law or practice, at any rate where the Strasbourg decision was made by a section rather than by the grand chamber.[79]

Another effect of the international origin of the rights is that domestic courts have treated them as subject to all limits applying in international law. This has caused problems relating to acts of UK public authorities outside the UK, as Strasbourg jurisprudence on the territorial reach of the ECHR is unclear. There is also a dispute as to whether military action under UN authority is attributable to the state or to the UN,

---

[73] Audit Commission, *Human Rights: Improving Public Service Delivery* (2003), paras 3, 12–13, available at *http://www.justice.gov.uk/guidance/humanrights.htm* (accessed 10 Oct. 2010).

[74] Parliamentary and Health Service Ombudsman, *Principles of Good Administration* (2009); Parliamentary and Health Service Ombudsman, *Principles for Remedy* (2009); Parliamentary and Health Service Ombudsman, *Principles of Good Complaint Handling* (2009), all available at *http://www.ombudsman.org.uk/improving-public-service/ombudsmansprinciples* (accessed 10 Oct. 2010).

[75] See further, David Feldman, 'Changes in Human Rights', in *Administrative Justice in Context*, ed. Michael Adler (Oxford, 2010), ch. 5.

[76] *R (Ullah)* v. *Special Adjudicator* [2004] UKHL 26, [2004] 2 AC 323, HL. Cf. Klug, *Values for a Godless Age*.

[77] *Kay* v. *Lambeth LBC* [2006] UKHL 10, [2006] 2 AC 465, HL; *Doherty* v. *Birmingham City Council (Secretary of State for Communities and Local Government intervening)* [2008] UKHL 57, [2009] AC 367, HL.

[78] *In re P* [2008] UKHL 38, *sub nom. In re G (Adoption: Unmarried Couple)* [2009] AC 173, HL.

[79] *R* v. *Horncastle* [2009] UKSC 14, [2010] 2 WLR 47, SC, declining to apply *Al-Khawaja and Tahery* v. *United Kingdom* (2009) 49 EHRR 1.

and whether the rights are subject to overriding authorisation given by, or under, UN Security Council resolutions adopted to maintain international peace and security under chapter 7 of the UN charter.[80]

Domestic courts have further restricted the scope of the act by declining the invitation to interpret 'public authority' in the light of a coherent view of the modern state. Instead, they have focused on whether there is anything about the service or facility provided (such as housing, or nursing care) that makes it distinctively appropriate for the public, rather than private, sector to take responsibility for it. The government has intervened to persuade them to change their approach, but with little success.[81] As a result, the impact of convention rights has been artificially narrowed,[82] and the outcomes of individual cases remain unpredictable.[83]

Some judges have also denied people the benefit of convention rights by reading section 6(2) of the act, designed to protect parliamentary sovereignty,[84] as overriding rights when statute confers a discretion, as well as when it imposes an obligation, on a public authority, and even where an authority is using common-law powers which operate alongside statutory regulation. This bizarre approach is part of a desperate attempt to save circuit judges from having to decide whether a possession order would be a justifiable interference with the right to respect for the home under Article 8 of the ECHR. Judgments of the Strasbourg court and the government's repeated interventions in litigation have so far failed to persuade judges to resile from what appears to be an untenable position.[85]

A development tending to extend, rather than restrict, the reach of convention rights has been the application of convention rights in proceedings where no public

[80] See, e.g., *R (Al-Skeini) v. Secretary of State for Defence (The Redress Trust intervening)* [2007] UKHL 26, [2008] AC 153, HL; *R (Al-Jedda) v. Secretary of State for Defence (JUSTICE intervening)* [2007] UKHL 58, [2008] AC 332, HL; *R (B.) v. Secretary of State for Foreign and Commonwealth Affairs* [2004] EWCA Civ 1314, [2005] QB 643, CA; *R (Gentle) v. Prime Minister* [2008] UKHL 20, [2008] AC 1356, HL; *R (Smith) v. Secretary of State for Defence* [2010] UKSC 29, SC; *R (Quark Fishing Ltd.) v. Secretary of State for Foreign and Commonwealth Affairs* [2005] UKHL 57, [2006] 1 AC 529, HL; *R (Bancoult) v. Secretary of State for Foreign and Commonwealth Affairs* [2008] UKHL 61, [2009] AC 453, HL.

[81] *YL v. Birmingham City Council* [2007] UKHL 27, [2008] 1 AC 95, HL. The immediate effect of the decision has been reversed by legislation: see Health and Social Care Act 2008, section 145; but the general approach still applies in other fields.

[82] See two reports by the Joint Committee on Human Rights, *The Meaning of Public Authority under the Human Rights Act*, Seventh Report of Session 2003–04, HL Paper 39, HC 382 (2004), and *The Meaning of Public Authority under the Human Rights Act,* Ninth Report of Session 2006–07, HL Paper 77, HC 410 (2007), and the government's response, *The Human Rights Act 1998: Definition of Public Authority – Government Response to the Joint Committee on Human Rights' Ninth Report of Session 2006–07*, Cm. 7726 (2009).

[83] E.g., compare *YL*, above, with *R (Weaver) v. London & Quadrant Housing Trust* [2009] EWCA Civ 587, [2010] 1 WLR 363, CA.

[84] Section 6(2) provides that it is not unlawful for a public authority to act incompatibly with a convention right 'if – (a) as the result of one or more provisions of primary legislation, the authority could not have acted differently, or (b) in the case of one or more provisions of, or made under, primary legislation which cannot be read or given effect in a way which is compatible with the Convention rights, the authority was acting so as to give effect to or enforce those provisions'.

[85] *Doherty v. Birmingham City Council* [2008] UKHL 57, [2008] 3 WLR 636, HL. But see now *Manchester City Council v. Pinnock (Secretary of State for Communities and Local Government and Equality and Human Rights Commission intervening)* [2010] UKSC 45, 3 Nov. 2010, esp. at paras [93]–[103], in which a nine-judged panel of the Supreme Court has reintroduced some rationality.

authority is involved. Courts have developed the law of breach of confidence so as to protect the right to private life under Article 8 of the ECHR, allowing it, in some cases, to outweigh the right to freedom of expression and the press under Article 10.[86] This is what supporters of the press hoped that section 12 of the act would avoid. It is not clear how the state's positive obligation to protect people's private life from intrusion comes to be enforceable in actions between private individuals, although 'judges of the highest authority have concluded that that follows from section 6(1) and (3) of the Human Rights Act 1998, placing on the courts the obligations appropriate to a public authority'.[87] But perhaps the best explanation was given by Sedley LJ: the obligation of courts under section 12 to have particular regard to freedom of expression is taken to mean the whole of Article 10, encompassing the grounds justifying interfering with that freedom in Article 10.2 as well as the right itself in Article 10.1. Among permitted grounds for restricting freedom of expression is the protection of the rights of others. This includes the right to respect for private life.[88] Simultaneously and unexpectedly, the Strasbourg court started treating states as having a duty to protect people (including celebrities) against unjustified invasion of their privacy by journalists.[89] As a result, the enactment of section 12 of the act has proved a pyrrhic victory for the press.

There are signs that the Strasbourg court may also be starting to intrude more on religious symbols in schools. In *Lautsi* v. *Italy*[90] a section held that states have an obligation of neutrality between religions to maintain diversity in education where one religion's adherents constitute a substantial majority in the state. The implications are not yet clear, and the case has been referred to the grand chamber. Nevertheless, it shows that Edward Leigh's concern about such matters, noted in section 3.3 above, was not without foundation.

On the other hand, remedial orders have not caused the constitutional damage which was feared. A fairly consistent practice has developed of legislating in response to a declaration of incompatibility, highlighting the tension between the ECHR and parliamentary sovereignty which Robert Maclennan identified (section 3.5 above). Yet remedial orders have hardly been used in practice, partly because the safeguards added in the Lords so slowed the process of making them that (save when the special procedure for urgent cases, without scrutiny in draft, can be used) it is usually quicker to use primary legislation. So far, only three remedial orders have been made.[91] However important the constitutional principles seemed, remedial orders have, as yet, had no observable effect on parliamentary sovereignty.

---

[86] *Campbell* v. *MGN Ltd.* [2004] UKHL 22, [2004] 2 AC 457, HL.

[87] *McKennitt* v. *Ash* [2006] EWCA Civ 1714; [2008] QB 73, CA, at para. [10] *per* Buxton LJ.

[88] *Douglas* v. *Hello! Ltd. (No. 1)* [2001] QB 967 at paras [132]–[136].

[89] *Von Hannover* v. *Germany* (2004) 40 EHRR 1. The case has returned to Strasbourg, where, at the time of writing, a public hearing is pending of the complaint that adjustments in domestic constitutional jurisprudence since 2004 have not adequately protected the complainants' right to respect for private life.

[90] (2010) 50 EHRR 42, Eur.Ct.HR. At the time of writing the grand chamber had held a public hearing but had not yet given judgment.

[91] See Joint Committee on Human Rights, *Making of Remedial Orders*, Seventh Report of Session 2001–02, HL Paper 58, HC 473 (2002); *English Public Law*, ed. David Feldman (2nd edn, 2009), 358–9.

4.3. *Human Rights in the Political Landscape*

The act became politically more controversial after the attack on the twin towers in 2001 caused heightened concern about security. The absolute nature of the right to freedom from torture has sometimes prevented the UK returning illegal immigrants or foreign suspected terrorists to countries where they face a real risk of torture, and has stopped (in theory, if not always in practice)[92] the security and intelligence services from co-operating with the US's programme of so-called 'extraordinary rendition' (kidnapping for the purpose of torture).

The Conservative Party in opposition wanted to respond by repealing the HRA and even denouncing the ECHR. Leading members of the Labour government, too, had become disenchanted with their child. Prime Minister Tony Blair, who had never been wholeheartedly convinced of its worth, exploited the threat of terrorism to decry the ECHR.[93] Some ministers recognized that realistically there was no escape from the ECHR. Nevertheless, they tried hard to persuade the Strasbourg court and domestic courts that the right to be free of torture could be interpreted as allowing states more leeway when dealing with non-European countries than in purely domestic matters.[94] Supporters of the HRA were on the back foot. The government proposed a review of the act as part of a wide-ranging review of the UK's whole system of government, provoked partly by the chaotic mismanagement when Mr Blair wanted to sack the lord chancellor, Lord Irvine, and was forced into major constitutional reform in the Constitutional Reform Act 2005.[95]

The government launched its programme of consultation in July 2007.[96] One object was to take more account of social and community interests which some claimed were being overwhelmed by individual rights. Consultation on human rights started in March 2009.[97] The government's idea was to restrict people's ability to insist on exercising rights in anti-social ways. There was to be no going back on the HRA and the ECHR (although the HRA might be incorporated into a bill of rights). Instead, the regime of rights would be developed beyond the ECHR, perhaps introducing non-justiciable social and economic rights, but with appropriate balancing mechanisms. The Conservative Party, by contrast, advocated replacing the HRA with a British bill of rights containing some rights which are absent from the ECHR, such as a right to jury trial, but limiting others, including the right to be free of torture.

The HRA received at least a temporary reprieve when the Conservatives failed to obtain an overall Commons' majority at the 2010 general election, and entered a

---

[92] See *R (Binyam Mohamed) v. Secretary of State for Foreign and Commonwealth Affairs* [2008] EWHC 2048 (Admin), [2008] EWHC 2100 (Admin), [2008] EWHC 2519 (Admin), [2009] EWHC 152 (Admin), [2009] EWHC 571 (Admin), [2009] EWHC 2549 (Admin), [2009] EWHC 2973 (Admin) (DC), [2010] EWCA Civ 65 and [2010] EWCA Civ 158 (CA).

[93] For discussion, see David Feldman, 'Human Rights, Terrorism and Risk: The Roles of Politicians and Judges', *Public Law* (2006), 364–84.

[94] E.g., the UK's intervention in *Saadi v. Italy*, Application No. 37201/06, judgment of 28 Feb. 2008 (GC), the home secretary's argument in *R (Wellington) v. Secretary of State for the Home Department* [2008] UKHL 72, [2009] AC 335, HL.

[95] Sir John Baker, 'Our Unwritten Constitution', *Proceedings of the British Academy*, clxvii (2010), 91, 96–7.

[96] Ministry of Justice, *The Governance of Britain*, Cm. 7170 (2007).

[97] Ministry of Justice, *Rights and Responsibilities: Developing our Constitutional Framework*, Cm. 7577 (2009).

coalition with the Liberal Democrats, who had always been the strongest supporters of the ECHR and the HRA. In a classic compromise, the two parties agreed to allow the future of the act to be reviewed by a commission, while accepting that it would have to build on the ECHR rather than detract from it.[98] This injects some realism, but it remains to be seen whether the act is safe in the long term: if Conservatives gain an overall majority at the next general election, they would be under considerable pressure to repeal it.

The act has had many useful effects, but its position remains insecure. Portrayed originally as part of a programme of constitutional reform, it has been hampered by the incoherence of subsequent reforms, some of which were unplanned, acts of panic and expediency, and chaotic, and by the weakness of public support for them. The last Labour government ultimately accepted the need for a public conversation to precede, rather than follow, constitutional change. As Professor Sir John Baker has said: 'The mad rush of the last seven years has proved to be the wrong approach. Constitutions must rest on a broad consensus, and we are some way from having any kind of consensus as to what is required.'[99] Its foundations in an international treaty have prevented it from becoming the British bill of rights for which supporters hoped: that remains a work in progress;[100] but it may yet prove to have been a significant step in that direction if the battle for hearts and minds can be won.

---

[98] HM Government, *Our Programme for Government: Freedom, Fairness, Responsibility* (2010), 11.

[99] Baker, 'Our Unwritten Constitution', 115. See further, Vernon Bogdanor, *The New British Constitution* (Oxford, 2009).

[100] Cf. Klug, *Values for a Godless Age*, and see Joint Committee on Human Rights, *A Bill of Rights for the UK?*, Twenty-ninth Report of Session 2007–08, HL Paper 165–I, HC 150–I (2008).

Enacting Scotland's 'Written Constitution': The Scotland Act 1998[*]

BARRY K. WINETROBE

The Scotland Act 1998 was one of the most significant pieces of constitutional legislation of the 1997–2010 Labour government. Yet, unlike the attempts to enact devolution in the 1970s, its parliamentary passage was relatively uncontroversial. In the 1970s, there was no party or public consensus for the proposed scheme, and no majority government to prevent various enforced amendments which ultimately led to its defeat in the March 1979 referendum. In the late 1990s, the situation was very different with much more consensus; a huge parliamentary majority with favourable legislative programming, and extensive advance policy development. The parliamentary progress of the bill was characterised by smooth passage and constructive scrutiny. Once enacted, the legislation was implemented smoothly and swiftly, though this did not prevent some unintended consequences, such as controversies over the Sewel convention and over the size of the Scottish parliament. The devolution scheme of the 1998 act enjoyed an extended honeymoon, with generally favourable political, financial and legal circumstances. However, recent years have seen the onset of more fluid and difficult times, which will test the robustness and viability of the 1998 act in the government of Scotland and of the United Kingdom.

Keywords: consensus; devolution; legislation; nationalism; parliament; policy making; implementation; referendum; Scotland; Scotland Bill; scrutiny

1. The Road to the Scotland Bill 1997–8

Scotland's distinctive form of governance in 1997 had been developing within the UK since 1707 and had intensified since the late 19th century through administrative devolution.[1] By the late 20th century, political scientists argued whether it was a political system, and whether the UK was a unitary, union or multi-national state.[2] In practice, there were three possible directions for Scotland's constitutional development – *status quo* Unionism, independence/separation or home rule/devolution Unionism.

A useful starting point is the perceived threat to the Labour Party in Scotland from the electoral rise of the Scottish National Party (SNP) in the late 1960s. This led to the Labour government's establishment of a royal commission on the constitution in 1969, with the implicit task of devising workable forms of devolution within a continuing United Kingdom.

[*] I am very grateful to all those colleagues who commented on earlier drafts of this article.

[1] J. Mitchell, *Governing Scotland* (Basingstoke, 2003).

[2] J. Kellas, *The Scottish Political System* (3rd edn, Cambridge, 1984); M. Keating and A. Midwinter, *The Government of Scotland* (Edinburgh, 1983).

The commission reported in 1973, with a range of constitutional proposals,[3] but the Conservative government under Edward Heath took no legislative action. However, the SNP's successes in the two 1974 general elections persuaded the returning Labour government that something had to be done. But attempting such complex and controversial constitutional reform with little or no parliamentary majority, and a bloc of back-bench rebels, proved to be difficult. Its Scotland and Wales Bill 1976–7 had to be abandoned when ministers could not force it through. The umbrella of the Lib-Lab Pact, which assured the minority government of Liberal support, saw a new attempt launched in 1977–8, with separate bills for Scotland and Wales.

That Scotland Bill had a long and difficult passage in both Houses,[4] with many amendments, some clearly 'wrecking', being forced on the government, including the imposition of the so-called '40% rule', requiring the referendum question to be supported by at least 40% of the total Scottish electorate. The 1 March 1979 referendum produced a very small majority in favour of activating the act (52% to 48%), but as the 'yes' vote constituted only 33% of the electorate, the proposition was rejected.

This provoked a successful no-confidence vote against the Labour government of James Callaghan on 28 March 1979, and, following the May 1979 general election, the new Conservative government repealed the act. During the following 18 years, ministers did not support devolution, but did initiate reforms, especially to Scottish business procedures at Westminster (by 1997, producing, in the enhanced Scottish grand committee, a Scottish mini-parliament in all but name at Westminster), and extending administrative devolution through the Scottish Office, all aimed at appeasing the growing pro-devolution tide.

Devolutionists concluded that any future campaign should be more people-driven.[5] This led eventually to the Scottish constitutional convention, comprising a wide range of civil society in Scotland. It laboured from 1989,[6] and provided a convenient backdrop for the two main participating parties, Labour and the Liberal Democrats, to negotiate agreements over sensitive aspects such as the size of, and voting system for, the proposed parliament. With this political backing, it was likely that the convention's final report, in November 1995, *Scotland's Parliament, Scotland's Right*, while not as comprehensive or rigorous as its proponents have sometimes claimed, would influence any new non-Conservative government's devolution policy.

The growing likelihood of a Labour government encouraged other devolution policy work. Three influential examples were the 1995 set of draft parliamentary procedures produced by Bernard Crick and David Millar,[7] and two constitution unit reports in 1996–7.[8] The latter are credited with persuading Labour to set out in the Scotland Bill

[3] *Royal Commission on the Constitution, 1969–1973. Vol. 1: Report*, Cmnd. 5460 (1973).

[4] P.D. Lindley, *The Scotland Act in Parliament: A Chronological Summary*, Civil Service College Working Paper No. 4 (1978); A.W. Bradley and D.J. Christie, *The Scotland Act 1978* (1979).

[5] A. Brown, 'Designing the Scottish Parliament', *Parliamentary Affairs*, liii (2000), 542; J. Mitchell, 'New Parliament, New Politics in Scotland', *Parliamentary Affairs*, liii (2000), 605.

[6] K. Wright, *The People Say Yes* (Glendareul, 1997).

[7] Bernard Crick and David Millar, *To Make the Parliament of Scotland a Model for Democracy* (Edinburgh, 1995); see also M. Mitchell, *Working Parliament for Scotland: Standing Orders for the Scottish Parliament* (Edinburgh, 1998).

[8] G. Leicester, *Scotland's Parliament: Fundamentals for a New Scotland Act* (1996); G. Leicester, *Illustrative Drafts for a New Scotland Bill* (1997).

a list of powers reserved to Westminster rather than (as in the 1978 act) the more cumbersome listing of powers devolved to the new parliament – a technical, but important, change.

The Labour Party under John Smith (1992–4) had committed itself to devolution and other constitutional proposals, an approach maintained, if less enthusiastically, by the next leader, Tony Blair. In both the Labour and the Liberal Democrats' 1997 election manifestos, legislation for devolution to Scotland (and Wales), was expressly made an early priority for a new government.

This was fulfilled by the introduction of the Referendums (Scotland and Wales) Bill as the 1997 parliament's first bill, with its second reading on 21–2 May. A week before its enactment on 31 July, the Scottish secretary, Donald Dewar, published a white paper, *Scotland's Parliament*,[9] containing more detail of what would be contained in the Scotland Bill, assuming a successful referendum result. The referendum was held on 11 September 1997, providing decisive majorities in favour of devolution and of limited tax-varying powers.

With all these preliminary obstacles successfully surmounted, the Scotland Bill itself – 116 clauses and eight schedules in 88 pages – was introduced in the Commons on 17 December 1997.[10] It began with the stark declaration: 'There shall be a Scottish Parliament' (clause 1(1)), to which Dewar added at its press launch in Glasgow the following day: 'I like that!'

2. *The Bill in Parliament*

Two broad features characterised the parliamentary journey of the Scotland Bill in the long 1997–8 session – smooth passage and constructive scrutiny.

2.1. *Smooth Passage*

For such a major, and potentially contentious, piece of legislation, and given the well-remembered parliamentary difficulties of the 1970s' devolution legislation, the Scotland Bill had a remarkably smooth passage through both houses of parliament. This was due to a conjunction of circumstances, not all planned, which diminished the nature and scale of opposition both to the bill in principle and to its specific provisions.

2.1.1. Party Arithmetic

The most obvious reason was the extent of Labour's landslide victory in the 1997 general election, with 418 seats to the Conservatives' 165. After 18 years in office, the tories' loss of nearly 180 seats was traumatic. Conversely, the doubling of the Liberal

---

[9] Scottish Office, *Scotland's Parliament*, Cm. 3658 (Edinburgh, 1997); Hansard, *Commons Debates*, 6th ser., ccxcviii, cols 1045–67: 24 July 1997.

[10] Bill 104 of 1997–8.

Democrat contingent to 46 gave them a strong pro-devolution voice. It was significant that Labour gained a clear majority of seats in England, with virtually double the number of tory seats, and their 328 English MPs all but providing a working majority themselves.

The Conservatives won no seats at all in Scotland and Wales, a huge blow, especially after managing, against expectations, to increase its representation in Scotland marginally in 1992. The Scottish and Welsh public's rejection of the Conservatives' largely *status quo* view of the union was clear.

2.1.2. Consensus

Labour and the Liberal Democrats had published a pre-election agreement,[11] under which they agreed to co-operate over a range of constitutional reforms including devolution. The Liberal Democrats, despite their opposition to a pre-legislative referendum, would not 'seek to frustrate or delay the referendum legislation', nor, following a successful result in the referendum, the main devolution legislation to be introduced in the first session.[12] Neither would the SNP, with six seats, though it wanted a multi-option referendum, to include an independence option, and much wider and deeper devolution than the government proposed.

Though not so clearly seen at the time, probably the most important factor in nullifying effective parliamentary opposition to the main devolution legislation was the result of the 1997 referendum. Labour's surprise announcement in June 1996 of a pre-legislative devolution referendum, including a separate question on a devolved parliament's tax-varying powers, was seen as a U-turn to pacify anti-devolutionists in the party and in the wider public, and to counter the Conservatives' claims that it would constitute a 'tartan tax'. Devolution supporters saw a referendum as unnecessary, and possibly designed by the Blair national leadership to fail, and some politicians and other commentators worried about the constitutional implications of a pre-legislative referendum.

However, the outcome of the referendum[13] unambiguously confirmed the support, seen indirectly in the recent general election, for the proposed devolution. The first, general question was supported by 74.3% of voters – 45% of the Scottish electorate, thereby surmounting even the infamous '40% rule' hurdle which defeated the 1979 referendum – and the financial question by 63.5% of voters. Parliament knew that the government's policy had a strong (Scottish) public mandate. This unequivocal public legitimation made outright opposition to the bill in either House practically impossible. Most opponents of the bill could thereafter offer only 'constructive opposition'.

This approach could be seen most clearly in the attitude of the Conservatives and the SNP. Both had refused to participate in the constitutional convention, the tories because they disagreed with devolution and the SNP (after some initial involvement) because the convention refused to discuss independence. However, both parties participated fully in

[11] *Report of the Joint Consultative Committee on Constitutional Reform* (Cook-Maclennan Agreement) (1997).
[12] Paras 39–40.
[13] D. Denver *et al.*, *Scotland Decides: The Devolution Issue and the 1997 Referendum* (2000).

the consultative steering group (CSG), set up by the Scottish Office in November 1997 to examine the practical and procedural operation of the parliament.

One tactic to finesse potential opposition was the surprise inclusion in the white paper of proposals which would lead to the reduction of the number of Scottish MPs.[14] Though logically not an 'answer' to what was termed the West Lothian question (or English question)[15] this provision diluted the potency of the representational and constitutional anomalies inherent in the devolution scheme, and which Tam Dalyell, the Labour member for West Lothian, had highlighted to great effect in the 1970s.[16]

2.1.3. Preparation

As noted, the Scottish constitution convention, and the cross-party negotiations on its fringes, contributed some components of a devolution scheme. After 1997, as well as the CSG itself, the new government set up other specialist groups and commissioned external research, designed to flesh out details of the overall policy. For example, the financial issues advisory group (FIAG), established in February 1998 and reporting a year later, examined issues that were dealt with in outline in the bill (section 70), and more fully in the Public Finance and Accountability (Scotland) Act 2000 (a Scottish act). Similarly, the topical issue of ethical standards in government was covered by a framework provision in the bill (section 39) prior to later detailed legislation and parliamentary mechanisms by the new parliament, following a report by a CSG code of conduct working group.

2.1.4. Procedural Context

The status of the proposed constitutional legislation, including the Scotland Bill, was much discussed prior to the 1997 election. As a 'constitutional bill' (an informal but recognized concept), as well as being a manifesto bill, it was argued that certain conventions applied to the Scotland Bill, including the taking of its Commons' committee stage entirely on the floor of the House; that it should not suffer guillotining, and that the house of lords adhere to the 'Salisbury convention' and not obstruct or defeat it or its main provisions.[17] However, there were suspicions that the new government would seek to bypass some or all of these claimed conventions,[18] and that the house of lords would seek to frustrate their plans, despite the Salisbury convention.

[14] *Scotland's Parliament*, Cm. 3658, para. 4.5. See section 86 of the 1998 act.

[15] *The English Question*, ed. R. Hazell (Manchester, 2006).

[16] T. Dalyell, *Devolution: The End of Britain?* (1977); House of Commons Library, Parliament and Constitution Centre, *The West Lothian Question*, Standard Note SN/PC/02586 (May 2010).

[17] J. Seaton and B. Winetrobe, 'The Passage of Constitutional Bills in Parliament', *Journal of Legislative Studies*, iv (1998), 33; R. Hazell, 'Time for a New Convention: Parliamentary Scrutiny of Constitutional Bills 1997–2005', *Public Law* (2006), 247.

[18] See Select Committee on Modernisation of the House of Commons, *The Legislative Process*, First Report of Session 1997–98, HC 190 (1997), esp. paras 57–66, 74–80.

Labour's 1997 manifesto had a significant package of proposed constitutional changes in addition to Scottish devolution, some of which inevitably overlapped with it. These included the parallel passage of Welsh and Northern Irish devolution legislation, notwithstanding the very significant differences in the three devolution schemes;[19] the Human Rights Bill; the promise of house of lords' reform, and 'modernisation' of Westminster procedure and practice, including the legislative process, which was assumed to be designed partly to ease the passage of government legislation.

All this required co-ordination, especially in the practicalities of parliamentary business management. Crucially, the territorial departments, rather than, as in the 1970s, a central department like the cabinet office or privy council office, would pilot their respective devolution bills. Donald Dewar, as Scottish secretary,[20] was a 'big hitter' with business management experience and influential cabinet support from chancellor of the exchequer, Gordon Brown and the lord chancellor, Lord Irvine (who chaired the cabinet's devolution committee), as well as the respect of the opposition parties. He had clear authority and status to drive through a policy to which he was personally committed.[21]

By being introduced relatively early in the first session, as promised in Labour's manifesto, the devolution legislation had the luxury of a potentially long session, until November or December 1998. Apart from other constitutional legislation, and several eye-catching social or economic bills (such as that on Bank of England independence), the legislative load in Labour's first session was relatively light.

Partly due to unexpectedly generous timetabling concessions by the Conservative opposition, which must have delighted government business managers, enabling a programme motion to be agreed for Commons' committee and later stages,[22] the bill was piloted through both Houses without resort to unilateral guillotining or any use of standing committees. There were only three Lords' defeats on amendments.[23] The bill passed all its stages on 17 November 1998, receiving royal assent two days later on the last day of the session. Because of the agreed timetabling, debate, though spread over almost a year, was often curtailed in the Commons, leaving many key issues to be more fully debated in the Lords. Of the approximately 190 hours of chamber time spent on the bill, nearly 107 hours were in Lords' proceedings, compared with just over 83 hours in the lower House (see table).

Though guillotined in the Commons, the passage of the referendum legislation in the summer of 1997, prior to the detailed scrutiny of the substantive devolution bills the following year, also amounted to a form of valuable pre-legislative scrutiny.

---

[19] Sometimes this crossover of parallel legislative provision was less expected, as in the arguments over 'open' or 'closed' lists for the regional portion of Scottish parliament elections (section 5), which was a key reason for the failure at the same time of the European Parliamentary Elections Bill 1997–8.

[20] As he had been chief whip in opposition, this was a deliberate appointment by Blair.

[21] For an insider view, see the chapters by Lords Irvine and Sewel in *Donald Dewar: Scotland's First First Minister*, ed. W. Alexander (Edinburgh, 2005).

[22] Hansard, *Commons Debates*, 6th ser., ccciv, cols 254–5: 13 Jan. 1998.

[23] *House of Lords Public Bill Sessional Statistics for Session 1997–98*, Table 12, available at http://www.publications.parliament.uk/pa/ld199798/ldpbstat/stat9813.htm (accessed 4 October 2010).

Table: *Parliamentary Stages of the Scotland Bill 1997–8*

Stage	Days	Dates	Bill no.
HC first reading	(formal)	17.12.97	104
HC second reading	2	12.1.98; 13.1.98	
HC committee of the whole House ('CWH')	8	28.1.98; 29.1.98; 10.2.98; 12.2.98; 23.2.98; 4.3.98; 30.3.98; 31.3.98	
HC report and third reading	3	6.5.98; 12.5.98; 19.5.98	166
HL first reading	(formal)	20.5.98	119
HL second reading	2	17.6.98; 18.6.98	
HL committee	10	8.7.98; 14.7.98; 16.7.98; 21.7.98; 23.7.98; 27.7.98; 28.7.98; 30.7.98; 6.10.98; 8.10.98	
HL report	4	22.10.98; 28.10.98; 2.11.98; 3.11.98	155
HL third reading	1	9.11.98	160
HC Lords' amendments	2	11.11.98; 16.11.98	256
HL Commons' amendments	1	17.11.98	165
Royal assent		19.11.98	Cap 46, 1998

2.2. *Constructive Scrutiny*

Parliamentary scrutiny was generally constructive, with much testing of the bill's core constitutional provisions. Confident of securing the ultimate passage of a bill in acceptable form, the government could afford to be relaxed about the nature and scope of particular topics of debate.

The bill, as passed in November 1998, at 132 clauses and nine schedules, was 16 clauses and one schedule larger than the original bill of the previous December. However, the act was not markedly different in its policy fundamentals, with virtually all significant changes being those proposed or agreed by the government. As the Scotland Bill 1997–8 is the biggest piece of constitutional legislation being examined in this volume, this section merely highlights three issues which arose in its passage, with others being examined in the next section's discussion on 'unintended consequences'.

2.2.1. Supremacy

The declaratory subclause in clause 27(7), and enacted unchanged as section 28(7) – 'This section does not affect the power of the Parliament of the United Kingdom to make laws for Scotland' – prompted serious debate on the nature of parliamentary sovereignty under devolution, something which the government insisted remained legally unchanged.[24] While some argued that this provision was unneces-

---

[24] *Scotland's Parliament*, Cm. 3658, para. 4.2: 'The UK Parliament is and will remain sovereign in all matters: but . . . Westminster will be choosing to exercise that sovereignty by devolving legislative responsibility to the Scottish Parliament without in any way diminishing its own powers.'

sary,[25] others sought to amend it to emphasize even further the continuing supremacy of the UK parliament, or to narrow it so as not to appear unnecessarily insulting to the new institutions. Examples of both unsuccessful approaches appeared at the very start of the Commons' committee stage on 28 January 1998.

The Conservatives moved amendments which explicitly declared the traditional constitutional doctrine of parliamentary supremacy, including a new subclause to clause 1 itself (which simply established the new parliament), ensuring that: 'the supreme authority of the parliament of the United Kingdom shall remain unaffected and undiminished over all persons, matters and things in Scotland'. Related amendments tried to expand clause 27(7) to apply the supremacy declaration not just to the section itself (which related to the parliament's law-making power) but to the whole act, and to make any amendment of UK acts beyond the parliament's legislative competence.

On the other hand, amendments from the Liberal Democrats and the SNP sought to restrict the supremacy declaration to UK legislation on 'reserved matters'. Assurances from Dewar, during the passing of the referendum legislation the previous year, that devolution would not legally prevent any future moves towards independence should that be the wish of the Scottish people, helped to keep the SNP on board.[26]

2.2.2. Finance

Inevitably, finance was a hotly-debated issue. The limited income tax-varying power in part 4 of the bill had long been controversial, whether as a 'step too far', or too feeble a fiscal power for a parliament. Arguably, the power was designed by the government to be largely symbolic rather than a significant policy lever for the devolved institutions, and its use – whether to raise or lower Scottish income tax – has never yet been seriously considered.

As well as the principle, many amendments sought to test the practicalities and mechanics of the proposals for grafting a devolved variation on what is essentially a UK-wide complex system of income tax law and practice. These included, for example, definitional issues, such as the meaning of a 'Scottish taxpayer' (in what became section 75)[27] and 'basic rate', and explicit restriction of the application of the power to levy income tax.[28]

Scrutiny of part 3 of the bill, dealing with more administrative arrangements for devolved finance, focused largely on the relationship between the two levels of government, and what many saw as entrenchment of the dependent nature and 'fiscal irresponsibility' of a devolved tier reliant almost totally on a central government block grant. The calculation, variation over time (via mechanisms such as the Barnett formula) and allocation of the central grant, as well as its impact on other parts of the UK, proved fertile debating material for both sides of the argument, even though little, if any, of this

---

[25] The first clause of the 1977–8 Scotland Bill, which contained a similar declaratory sovereignty provision, was removed after being defeated in the Commons: Hansard, *Commons Debates*, 5th ser., cmxxxix, cols 1323–409: 22 Nov. 1977.

[26] E.g., see Hansard, *Commons Debates*, 6th ser., ccxciv, col. 725: 21 May 1997.

[27] Hansard, *Commons Debates*, 6th ser., cccvii, cols 91–109: 23 Feb. 1998; Hansard, *Lords Debates*, 5th ser., dxciii, cols 2056–9: 28 Oct. 1998.

[28] Hansard, *Lords Debates*, 5th ser., dxciii, cols 261–81: 6 Oct. 1998.

crucial detail was actually in the bill itself.[29] Finally, the technical provisions for account-ing and audit of devolved finance also provided scope for discussion of the proper nature and extent, if any, of Westminster/Whitehall oversight of, or even control over, the use by the devolved institutions of their grant, either directly or by determining the mechanisms of the devolved institutions' own financial control.[30]

2.2.3. The Judiciary and Legal System

It was inevitable that the courts and their judges would become more prominent under Labour's constitutional reforms, including, as we have seen, the Human Rights Act 1998. So, too, with the Scotland Bill, as a 'written constitution' for devolved Scotland, with the transformation of much convention and practice into statute, and the judges armed with enhanced review over devolved legislation. 'The judiciary is at the centre of the legal system, and the legal system is at the heart of the Scottish difference that justifies devolution.'[31] Two aspects illustrate how Westminster dealt with these matters during scrutiny of the bill:

• *Appointment and Removal of Scottish Judges*[32]

The opportunity was taken to 'codify' such arrangements as existed for the appointment and removal of judges, by allocating responsibility between the devolved and reserved tiers. There had been relatively little detail in the white paper,[33] or the bill as intro-duced.[34] Ministers did not expect the extent of challenge to this clause, though that this was largely concentrated in the house of lords was itself not so surprising, given that House's legal experience.

Some of this was briefly rehearsed in the Commons,[35] where the government made some concessions, especially on the removal provisions.[36] The more sustained challenge in the Lords led to the inclusion, against the government's wishes, of a totally new 'independent tribunal' element into the removal process.[37] The government accepted this defeat,[38] bringing in its own version, mainly during the Lords' amendments stage in the Commons.[39] Devolved Scotland has since made its own provision in many of these areas,

[29] Hansard, *Commons Debates*, 6th ser., cccvi, cols 566–609: 12 Feb. 1998; Hansard, *Lords Debates*, 5th ser., dxcii, cols 1654–80: 30 July 1998.

[30] Hansard, *Commons Debates*, 6th ser., cccvi, cols 610–41: 12 Feb. 1998; Hansard, *Lords Debates*, 5th ser., dxcii, cols 1712–22: 30 July 1998.

[31] Dewar, second reading speech: Hansard, *Commons Debates*, 6th ser., ccciv, col. 30: 12 Jan. 1998.

[32] C. Himsworth, 'Securing the Tenure of Judges: A Somewhat Academic Exercise?', *Public Law* (1999), 14.

[33] *Scotland's Parliament*, Cm. 3658, para. 2.4.

[34] Clause 89 on appointment (including the prime minister's role in respect of the lord president and the lord justice clerk) and on removal.

[35] See, e.g., the committee debate: Hansard, *Commons Debates*, 6th ser., cccvii, cols 1150–60: 4 Mar. 1998.

[36] Hansard, *Commons Debates*, 6th ser., cccxii, cols 777–85: 19 May 1998.

[37] Hansard, *Lords Debates*, 5th ser., dxciv, cols 41–72: 2 Nov. 1998 (opposition amendment carried, 144 to 108).

[38] Third reading: Hansard, *Lords Debates*, 5th ser., dxciv, cols 586–92: 9 Nov. 1998.

[39] Hansard, *Commons Debates*, 6th ser., cccxix, cols 440–57: 11 Nov. 1998.

with a non-statutory Judicial Appointments Board in 2002, and in the Judiciary and Courts (Scotland) Act 2008.

- *'Constitutional Court'*

The selection of the judicial committee of the privy council (JCPC) as ultimate legal arbiter of devolution disputes, rather than the house of lords or a new constitutional court, was controversial.[40] There was much debate over the appropriate membership of the JCPC in its devolution role, with the government widening its original white paper proposals in clause 94 of the bill,[41] but successfully resisting attempts in the Lords to broaden it even further beyond UK judges to include senior Commonwealth judges.[42]

Both Houses debated the creation of some form of new 'constitutional court', to reflect the new constitutional environment generally. Alex Salmond, the SNP leader, unsuccessfully moved a new clause at Commons' report stage for a court based on the German model.[43] At Lords' report stage, a Liberal Democrat amendment for a constitutional court of a different design was debated,[44] but later withdrawn.

Ministerial resistance to these proposals, and defence of the JCPC as the appropriate forum for devolution dispute resolution, soon rang rather hollow with the sudden emergence, as part of the fallout of a botched ministerial reshuffle in June 2003, of the government's proposal for a UK supreme court, which would absorb the JCPC's devolution jurisdiction.[45]

2.2.4. 'Niche scrutiny'

While the bill itself was taken wholly on the floor of both Houses, it, and the policy issues contained within it, were also the subject of some important committee scrutiny.

In November 1997, the Scottish affairs committee announced an inquiry into 'the operation of multi-layer democracy', and its report was published on 2 December 1998, shortly after royal assent.[46] This inquiry, concurrent with the passage of the bill, examined many constitutional and practical issues, such as the stability of the new and complex arrangements, often from a valuable comparative perspective.

In the Lords, the delegated powers and deregulation committee, which examines bills for any inappropriate provision, or inadequate parliamentary scrutiny, of delegated

---

[40] C. Boyd, 'Parliament and Courts: Powers and Disputes Resolution' and G. Jackson, 'Devolution and the Scottish Legal Institutions', in *Devolution to Scotland: the Legal Aspects*, ed. T. StJ. Bates (Edinburgh, 1997).

[41] *Scotland's Parliament*, Cm. 3658, para. 4.17.

[42] See third reading: Hansard, *Lords Debates*, 5th ser., dxciv, cols 592–8: 9 Nov. 1998.

[43] Hansard, *Commons Debates*, 6th ser., cccxii, cols 204–13: 12 May 1998. The new clause was defeated, 8 to 388.

[44] Hansard, *Lords Debates*, 5th ser., dxciii, cols 1963–86: 28 Oct. 1998.

[45] Ultimately enacted in the Constitutional Reform Act 2005.

[46] Scottish Affairs Committee, *The Operation of Multi-Layer Democracy*, Second Report of Session 1997–98, HC 460 (1998).

legislative power, twice scrutinised the Scotland Bill.[47] Its recommendations led to substantial rewriting of the bill's subordinate legislation provisions.[48]

3. *Scotland Act 1998: Consequences and Legacy*

3.1. *Delivery*

In terms of major constitutional change, the devolution scheme was implemented swiftly. Just two years after the Labour government took office, the Scottish parliament's first elections were held on 6 May 1999 (under an additional member system of voting, combining a simple plurality constituency, with multi-member top-up regions). The parliament met for the first time on 12 May. A Labour-Liberal Democrat coalition agreement was speedily concluded and a ministerial team appointed. The new devolved institutions (which had already been operating since mid-May) gained their full legislative and executive powers on 1 July (D-day), symbolised by a royal 'state opening' at the parliament. Many of the factors described in the previous section as easing the parliamentary passage of the legislation also assisted in this rapid, and relatively smooth, implementation.

While the act itself was necessary to the new devolved system, it would not be, by itself, sufficient.[49] In keeping with the spirit of devolving power from the centre, much of the act, and its attendant subordinate legislation, was intended to be either of a framework or temporary nature, so that the new devolved institutions could both flesh out and amend its provisions in many areas, such as the procedures and practices of the new parliament.

This was not limited to the consequential delegated legislation fleshing out the statutory scheme, and further amending or new primary legislation by both the UK and Scottish parliaments. It included the new parliament's standing orders, and other procedural guidance; the executive's guidance;[50] and the UK government's devolution guidance, including concordats.

With such a complex and diverse collection of material, which collectively provide much of the 'written constitution' of devolved Scottish governance, and potentially contradictory aims and objectives, the scope for inconsistency is great. To some extent, this was mitigated by the close involvement, in the 1997–9 period, of the old Scottish Office and its officials, with most of those closely involved moving to the new devolved institutions.[51] With hindsight, it can be seen that more detailed and considered thought had been given to the establishment of the parliament than to the transformation of the

---

[47] House of Lords Delegated Powers and Deregulation Committee, Twenty-fourth Report of Session 1997–98, HL Paper 124 (1998); Thirty-second Report of Session 1997–98, HL Paper 146 (1998). Had they been in existence at that time, the house of lords' constitution committee and the joint committee on human rights would probably also have undertaken relevant 'niche scrutiny' of the bill.

[48] Esp. sections 112–15 and schedule 7.

[49] It said very little, e.g., about any impacts on the European and local government tiers.

[50] E.g., Scottish Executive, *Scottish Ministerial Code*, and *Guide to Collective Decision Making* (Edinburgh, 1999).

[51] P. Grice, 'The Creation of a Devolved Parliament', *Journal of Legislative Studies*, vii (2001), 1.

Scottish Office into the brand-new devolved Scottish executive and a residual UK department, the Scotland Office.[52]

3.2. *Unintended Consequences*

It would be unrealistic to expect such a large and complex piece of constitutional legislation to be implemented without the need for modification. Inevitably, its provisions would produce unintended consequences, some unforeseen, others whose scale and impact were underestimated. Three examples are briefly summarized here.

3.2.1. The Sewel Convention[53]

Despite the granting of legislative power to the new parliament, the 1997 white paper noted that there may be occasions: 'where it will be more convenient for legislation to be passed by the UK parliament'.[54] A Scottish Office minister, Lord Sewel, in July 1998, fleshed this out during discussion of the supremacy clause: 'we would expect a convention to be established that Westminster would not normally legislate with regard to devolved matters in Scotland without the consent of the Scottish parliament'.[55]

There was no suggestion that the UK (or, a future Scottish) government would regard the proposed convention as a positive trigger for Westminster legislating in devolved areas. However, from 1999, use of so-called 'Sewel motions' (by which the Scottish parliament granted consent to a UK government request that Westminster legislates in a specified area), far from being limited to what first minister, Donald Dewar, described as 'exceptional and limited circumstances',[56] appeared to be virtually a matter of routine, government-driven and subject to inadequate parliamentary oversight. The perception of Westminster muscling into Holyrood's legislative space, especially in controversial areas, was palpable and destabilising.

Both parliaments and governments reviewed this issue,[57] and more transparent and accountable processes were introduced. While not much reducing the frequency of what are now known as legislative consent motions, even under an SNP government, they appear to have taken the heat out the issue.

---

[52] R. Parry, 'Changing UK Governance under Devolution', *Public Policy and Administration*, xxiii (2008), 114; R. Pyper, 'The Civil Service: A Neglected Dimension of Devolution', *Public Money and Management*, xix (1999), 45; M. Keating and P. Cairney, 'A New Elite? Politicians and Civil Servants in Scotland after Devolution', *Parliamentary Affairs*, lix (2006), 43.

[53] B. Winetrobe, 'A Partnership of the Parliaments: Scottish Law Making under the Sewel Convention at Westminster and Holyrood', in *Devolution, Law Making and the Constitution*, ed. R. Hazell and R. Rawlings (Exeter, 2005).

[54] *Scotland's Parliament*, Cm. 3658, para. 4.4.

[55] Hansard, *Lords Debates*, 5th ser., dxcii, col. 791: 21 July 1998.

[56] Scottish Parliament Official Report, 16 June 1999, c 403.

[57] These include: Scottish Parliament Procedures Committee, 7th Report 2005, *The Sewel Convention*, SP Paper 428 (2005); House of Commons Scottish Affairs Committee, *The Sewel Convention: The Westminster Perspective*, Fourth Report of Session 2005–06, HC 983 (2006).

3.2.2. Size of the Scottish Parliament

As already noted, one 'answer' to the West Lothian question was the reduction in the number of Scottish MPs. However, as the bill was drafted, this would have an automatic knock-on effect in the number of Scottish parliament seats, reducing them from 129 to around 104–8. An amendment carried against the government in the Lords to retain the parliament's original size[58] was overturned in the Commons.[59]

However, in the Lords on 17 November, Lord Sewel did hint that the issue could be revisited in the light of experience.[60] Sure enough, pressure for retention of a 129-seat parliament grew so that the government conceded a review in November 2001,[61] and the following month published a consultation paper.[62] A year later, the predictable U-turn was confirmed,[63] and the bill amending the 1998 act passed in 2004.[64]

3.2.3. Constitutional Watchdogs[65]

As early as second reading, David Davis (public accounts committee chair) had described as 'extremely weak' the provisions in clause 66(1)(c) establishing 'an independent person' to undertake core financial accounting and audit tasks.[66] In committee, he introduced amendments, derived from the National Audit Act 1983's comptroller and auditor general provisions, seeking to provide greater independence from government in that person's appointment and removal. Ministers responded positively, and at report stage moved amendments which eventually became section 69, creating the post of auditor general for Scotland, appointed by the monarch on nomination of the parliament, and removable by her after a parliamentary resolution, supported by two-thirds of all MSPs (members of the Scottish parliament).[67]

This apparently innocuous provision became the template for the parliament's creation of six other devolved 'parliamentary commissioners', such as the Scottish information commissioner, whose governance, financing and accountability, through it, and its own governing body, the Scottish parliamentary corporate body (SPCB), have been continuously controversial, generating several inquiries on their governance arrangements.[68]

[58] Hansard, *Lords Debates*, 5th ser., dxci, cols 1331–40: 8 July 1998; dxciii, cols 1591–1607: 22 Oct. 1998 (amendment carried, 103 to 94).

[59] Hansard, *Commons Debates*, 6th ser., cccxix, cols 377–405: 11 Nov. 1998 (Lords' amendments disagreed, 303 to 173); accepted by the Lords: Hansard, *Lords Debates*, 5th ser., dxciv, cols 1180–96: 17 Nov. 1998 (opposition motion defeated, 53 to 119).

[60] Hansard, *Lords Debates*, 5th ser., dxciv, col. 1195: 17 Nov. 1998.

[61] Hansard, *Commons Debates*, 6th ser., ccclxxiv, col. 91: 6 Nov. 2001.

[62] Scotland Office, *The Size of the Scottish Parliament* (2001).

[63] Hansard, *Commons Debates*, 6th ser., cccxcvi, cols 859–71: 18 Dec. 2002.

[64] Scottish Parliament (Constituencies) Act 2004.

[65] O. Gay and B. Winetrobe, *Officers of Parliament: Transforming the Role* (2003), Part 3; *Parliament's Watchdogs: At the Crossroads*, ed. O. Gay and B. Winetrobe (2008), ch. 3.

[66] Hansard, *Commons Debates*, 6th ser., ccciv, col. 69: 12 Jan. 1998.

[67] Hansard, *Commons Debates*, 6th ser., cccxii, cols 761–6: 19 May 1998.

[68] The latest, at the time of writing, being the Review of SPCB Supported Bodies Committee, *1st Report, 2009*, SP Paper 266 (Edinburgh, 2009).

3.3. *Conclusion*

Devolution, including the Scotland Act 1998 scheme, can be regarded either as a 'settlement' (the Labour government's view), or a 'process, not an event' (the phrase used by both the former Welsh secretary, Ron Davies,[69] and by Dewar). While no scheme of constitutional governance can be static or final, the 'settlement' view suggests consensus around a robust and effective reform designed to last, with minimal, incremental change.

For both anti-devolutionists and some nationalists, devolution is a stepping stone, itself fuelling, rather than diminishing, the drive towards independence. For such nationalists, it is a 'win-win' situation. If devolution is seen as successful within its limitations, it enhances the Scottish public's desire for greater self-government, or its very limitations can be blamed for any failure, with the same result. The Unionist anti-devolutionist line was best expressed by the then Labour MP, Tam Dalyell: 'Whatever else it is, the [1997–8 Scotland] Bill is not a settlement . . . I see no reason to retract the view that I expressed constantly and daily during the referendum, that, unfortunately, we are on a motorway without exit to an independent state.'[70]

Viewing devolution as a process does not necessarily buy into the 'stepping stone to independence' view, but recognizes that major constitutional change will inevitably need refining and developing with experience, within the fundamental parameters of the settlement, of 'devolution within the UK'. Some see the devolved institutions gaining more legislative and financial powers, or even new constitutional arrangements within the union, such as federalism.[71] Others prefer the process to be a 'rolling programme'[72] of tweaking and reinforcing the present arrangements.

Since 1999, despite political and presentational crises,[73] Scottish devolution has enjoyed a remarkably smooth ride, a much-extended honeymoon.[74] This is largely due to three factors:

- like-minded governments in London and Edinburgh;
- benign economic and financial conditions enabling the delivery of popular but costly (and, in England, controversial) policies, such as on personal care for the elderly and student finance; and
- no seriously destabilising legal or political challenges to the scheme.

More recently, the first two factors have changed, with the election in 2007 of a SNP minority government in Scotland, and the impact of the recession and tighter public

[69] R. Davies, *Devolution: A Process Not an Event*, Gregynog Papers 2.2, Institute of Welsh Affairs (Cardiff, 1999).

[70] Hansard, *Commons Debates*, 6th ser., cccvii, cols 1080–1: 4 Mar. 1998.

[71] The Steel Commission, *Moving to Federalism: A New Settlement for Scotland*, Report to the Scottish Liberal Democrat Spring Conference (Edinburgh, 2006).

[72] R. Hazell, 'The UK's Rolling Program of Devolution: Slippery Slope or Safeguard of the Union?', in *Reforming Parliamentary Democracy*, ed. F Seidle and D Docherty (Montreal, 2003), 180.

[73] The difficulties with the building of the new parliamentary complex at Holyrood being the prime example.

[74] B. Winetrobe, 'Scottish Devolution: Developing Practice in Multi-layer Governance', in *The Changing Constitution*, ed. J. Jowell and D. Oliver (6th edn, Oxford, 2007).

spending, and these changes may also provoke more serious legal and political challenges to the present scheme.[75]

The 2007 Holyrood election result transformed the Scottish constitutional debate. Events in Wales over recent years have demonstrated that a devolution 'settlement', albeit one rather different from that in Scotland, can be significantly amended due to public and political pressure, even where there was initially little indication of UK government willingness to revisit the issue.[76]

One major review of devolution and options for the future of Scottish governance has now been completed,[77] and the SNP government has embarked on another.[78] Westminster committees have also reviewed various aspects of the overall devolution schemes over the years.[79]

Subject to any patent and unanswerable demand for independence through a referendum or election, any UK-driven changes will be presented as a logical development of the existing successful devolution 'settlement', consistent with maintenance of the union. That any return to a pre-1999 situation, with the abolition of the Scottish parliament and government, is virtually inconceivable, shows that, to that extent at least, the Scotland Act 1998 devolution scheme can be regarded as a success in Scotland.

Scottish devolution is not just a Scottish issue. The UK perspective is fundamental to the development of Scottish territorial governance, and the priorities and imperatives of a centre which ultimately controls the devolution scheme, will continue to have a huge, even decisive, say in the future.[80] This is not just the familiar issue of constitutional asymmetry, such as the West Lothian/English question or the Barnett formula. So long as the UK centre's overriding imperative is the maintenance of a United Kingdom which includes Scotland, that will be the fundamental policy yardstick by which any territorial governance proposals will be measured.

Devolution came about in Scotland in the late 1990s for a number of reasons, including overall constitutional 'modernisation'; more decentralised and democratically-accountable government;[81] a 'not like Westminster' form of 'new politics',[82] and a political response to demands for change in Scottish governance (especially the perceived threat

---

[75] A. Trench, 'Scotland and Wales: The Evolution of Devolution', in *Constitutional Futures Revisited: Britain's Constitution to 2020*, ed. R. Hazell (Basingstoke, 2008).

[76] *Report of the Richard Commission on the Powers and Electoral Arrangements of the National Assembly for Wales* (Cardiff, 2004); Government of Wales Act 2006.

[77] The Scottish parliament/UK government-supported Calman Commission, which reported in June 2009: Commission on Scottish Devolution, *Serving Scotland Better: Scotland and the United Kingdom in the 21st Century*, Final Report (Edinburgh, 2009).

[78] The Scottish National Party government's 'national conversation'.

[79] The most recent being those of the House of Commons Justice Committee, *Devolution: A Decade On*, Fifth Report of Session 2008–09, HC 529–1 (2009), and the House of Lords Select Committee on the Barnett Formula, *The Barnett Formula*, 1st Report of Session 2008–09, HL Paper 139 (2009).

[80] For the purposes of this article, potential European drivers for change are not examined.

[81] M. Keating *et al.*, 'Does Devolution Make a Difference? Legislative Output and Policy Divergence in Scotland', *Journal of Legislative Studies*, ix (2003), 110.

[82] Precedents in the 1998 act can later be used in a UK context, as in carryover of provisions thought appropriate for a sub-national, statutory parliament to the parliament at Westminster, as in the attempted creation of statutory regulation of parliamentary standards in the Parliamentary Standards Act 2009.

to the union of Scottish nationalism).[83] Scottish devolution since 1999 has been relatively stable and popular, and, in terms of these political and constitutional reasons just outlined, relatively successful.

Whether or not success can be finally pronounced after a decade depends largely on whether or not the first decade turns out to have been an extended honeymoon where any major flaws or gaps in the scheme have yet to be discovered or tested. If fissures emerge of greater political and economic challenges, this may be evidence of lack of robustness in the 1998 act scheme, such as its implicit assumption, typical of New Labour hubris in the late 1990s, of permanent comity of political control in London and Edinburgh.

Despite some superficiality and gaps in Westminster's scrutiny of the Scotland Bill, which may account for the various unintended consequences and remaining unfinished business, it can claim at least some credit for this generally positive evaluation of the success of the legislative scheme. However, the Welsh experience demonstrates that such scrutiny is not in itself sufficient guarantee of success. This suggests that there were other factors at play in the 'quality' of the Scottish devolution legislation, many of which were outlined above in the sections on smooth passage and constructive scrutiny. There may be lessons here for governments, parliaments and the public for the preparation and parliamentary scrutiny of any future constitutional legislation.

[83] S. Tierney, 'Giving with One Hand: Scottish Devolution Within a Unitary State', *International Journal of Constitutional Law*, v (2007), 572–97.

Stages and Muddles: The House of Lords Act 1999

ALEXANDRA KELSO

As one of the most significant pieces of constitutional legislation enacted in the last century, the House of Lords Act 1999 radically reformed the membership of the second chamber of the Westminster parliament by removing almost all the hereditary peers who sat there. The act formed a key part of the constitutional reform agenda of the Labour government elected in 1997, but despite its massive majority in the house of commons, eliminating the hereditary peerage proved far harder than might first have been imagined. This article seeks to explore the events surrounding that act, the political machinations and deals leading up to it, the course of the legislation through parliament, and the intricacies of the process involved in securing constitutional reform of this magnitude. It concludes by examining the consequences of the act for subsequent attempts at further second chamber reform during the rest of the Labour government's time in office.

Keywords: Conservative Party; elected upper House; hereditary peers; House of Lords Bill; Labour government; legislation; parliament; royal commission on reform of the house of lords; Weatherill amendment

The House of Lords Act 1999 was one of the most significant pieces of constitutional legislation enacted during the 20th century, hence its inclusion in this volume, and it (partially) fulfilled a goal that persisted as a key part of the Lords' reform agenda since the Parliament Act 1911: that is, the removal of the hereditary peers from the second chamber. In locating the act within the context of a two-stage approach to Lords' reform, the Labour government believed it could remove the most democratically-offensive part of the chamber, and then proceed to identify a clear position with respect to compositional reform behind which the party could unite. However, the decade that followed the act was marked by policy uncertainty and confusion, which rendered the subsequent processes of Lords' reform muddled and rudderless, and, ironically, undermined what was, in fact, a major constitutional change with lasting and substantial consequences for Westminster politics.

1. *The Rationale for Reform*

The Labour Party has, throughout its history, had a highly-changeable policy towards the house of lords, and as late as 1983 was committed in its general election manifesto to abolishing the chamber altogether, and to redesigning Westminster as a unicameral parliament.[1] The Conservative-dominated hereditary peerage in the upper chamber

---

[1] Labour Party, *The New Hope for Britain* (1983).

proved in the post-war era to be a source of considerable frustration to Labour governments, both on points of policy and on points of principle. Not only did a hereditary chamber offend the democratising instincts of the Labour Party, but the substantially-outnumbered Labour peers in the Lords found themselves easily voted down, regardless of the value of the legislative points they sought to make.[2] In the 1970s and 1980s, the general view held in the Labour Party was that a second chamber could too easily frustrate the wishes of a committed government of the left, and that, rather than expend energy and political capital on reforming it, the far more sensible option was to simply abolish the upper House, and focus, instead, on reforming the various practices and procedures of the democratically-elected lower House in which the government sat.

By 1992, however, the party's policy had changed markedly, and unicameralism was abandoned in favour of support for an elected upper House.[3] This modification reflected a growing commitment within the Labour Party to constitutional change more broadly, spearheaded by Labour leader, John Smith, and demonstrated by the, then, shadow chancellor, Gordon Brown, arguing for a new constitutional settlement that comprised reform of the 'indefensible' unelected Lords, but which also mapped out increasingly coherent plans for devolution, incorporation of the European Convention on Human Rights (ECHR), and freedom of information.[4] By 1997, these plans had become even further embedded into the Labour Party's policy infrastructure, and the commitment to 'cleaning up' politics and facilitating democratic renewal formed a cornerstone of the New Labour brand promoted by Tony Blair and Gordon Brown. Policy commitments on the house of lords received considerably more space in the 1997 manifesto than in previous years, yet also demonstrated that yet another shift in emphasis had occurred since 1992:

> The House of Lords must be reformed. As an initial, self-contained reform, not dependent on further reform in the future, the right of hereditary peers to sit and vote in the House of Lords will be ended by statute. This will be the first stage in a process of reform to make the House of Lords more democratic and representa- tive . . . A committee of both Houses of Parliament will be appointed to undertake a wide-ranging review of possible further change and then to bring forward proposals for reform.[5]

The fundamental point to note with respect to the 1997 Labour Party manifesto, then, is that it said nothing about the need to create an elected second chamber. The commitment to reform was restricted to getting rid of the hereditary peers. Whereas the 1992 manifesto clearly stated the party's intent to create an elected House, the 1997 manifesto said nothing of the sort, instead using the rather less explicit language about making the chamber 'more democratic and representative', but avoiding entirely any

---

[2] Michael Wheeler-Booth, 'The House of Lords', in R. Blackburn *et al.*, *Griffith and Ryle on Parliament: Functions, Practice and Procedure* (2003).

[3] Labour Party, *It's Time to Get Britain Working Again* (1992).

[4] G. Brown, 'The Servant State: Towards a New Constitutional Settlement', *Political Quarterly*, lxiii (1992), 394–403.

[5] Labour Party, *New Labour: Because Britain Deserves Better* (1997).

declared statement of what this might mean in practice. The pragmatism of the manifesto was that it substantially shifted the reform terrain by committing to a two-stage process. For most of the 20th century, debates about house of lords' reform were plagued by a contradictory certainty: certainty that the hereditary principle was indefensible in the context of a modern representative democracy, and the concomitant certainty that no one could agree on what should replace it. By 1997, the Labour leadership had decided that the one way to get beyond this impasse was simply to abolish the right of the hereditary peers to sit and vote in parliament, and thus eradicate the most offensive aspect of the upper chamber, and only then start thinking about the far trickier matter of broader compositional reform. The new house of lords' policy also indicated that removing the hereditary peers did not mean that further reform was either necessary or guaranteed, a position that would be a source of considerable political annoyance for the party once in power.

As far as house of lords' reform was concerned, then, the 1997 Labour Party manifesto, and its two-stage approach, was a masterclass in political realism. It acknowledged the lessons of the past 100 years, and the failure to find agreement on what a reformed composition should look like, but committed, nevertheless, to removing the hereditary peers, and thus easily demonstrating the incoming government's democratic credentials. The Labour Party had already tried in government to proceed with holistic second chamber reform in 1968–9,[6] and to do so in a cross-party fashion, an endeavour which had ended in failure and embarrassment. If it wished to secure any kind of reform, then, it needed to be able to do so by relying only on the support of its own members. A two-stage approach enabled a future Labour government to take advantage of the support within its own party for removing the hereditary peers, and only then think about a cross-party basis for future reform once that first bridge had been successfully crossed. Indeed, simply getting rid of the hereditary peers seemed like a relatively straightforward piece of constitutional reform, given how hard it had become to defend the hereditary principle. Yet, as the Labour government found out, it was neither easy nor straightforward, and crucially, it was not without political costs.

Having been out of office for almost two decades, the new Labour government elected in 1997 had a substantial programme of reform it wished to implement, and its constitutional change agenda was, arguably, unlike any that had ever before been pursued by an incoming administration. Consequently, with its capacity for action initially constrained by what could be secured in terms of legislation in the first parliamentary session, the government necessarily had to decide upon its commitments, and by far the most important of its constitutional policies was devolution and, to a lesser extent, human rights. As a result, a significant portion of the first session of 1997–8 was accounted for by legislating for these policies,[7] and the cabinet decided that reform of the house of lords would be delayed until the second session of 1998–9. The decision to delay was a key determining factor in the subsequent course of house of lords' reform. The magnitude of the defeat suffered by the Conservative Party in 1997 left it in a state of stunned disarray in the house of commons, and in almost no position to offer meaningful opposition to

[6] See Janet P. Morgan, *The House of Lords and the Labour Government 1964–1970* (Oxford, 1975), ch. 8.

[7] See Matthew Flinders, 'The Half-hearted Constitutional Revolution', in *Developments in British Politics 8*, ed. P. Dunleavy *et al.* (Basingstoke, 2006).

anything that the Labour government proposed in its first year.[8] It is very likely that, had the government proceeded to legislate for the removal of the hereditary peers in its first parliamentary session in power, the story of the House of Lords Act recounted here would be rather different. As it was, however, the government did delay, and in so doing, allowed the Conservative opposition time to catch its breath and prepare for battle.

2. *Negotiating the Reform Process*

Action to fulfil the manifesto commitment began with the 1998 queen's speech, which promised a bill 'to remove the right of hereditary Peers to sit and vote in the House of Lords', with the stipulation once more being made that this would be 'the first stage in a process of reform to make the House of Lords more democratic and representative'.[9] The queen's speech also diverged from what had been promised in the manifesto, by announcing the establishment of a royal commission 'to review further changes and speedily to bring forward proposals for reform'. The manifesto had, in fact, pledged a joint committee of both Houses, which is a quite different institutional creature from a royal commission, with the latter traditionally taking far longer to reach agreed reports, and also being somewhat easier for governments to manage because of the different dynamics of the power of appointment.

The government's plan to remove the hereditary peers and only then consider further compositional reform of the upper chamber may well have been the best option in terms of actually securing change, but it, nevertheless, afforded the opposition a prime strategy for attack. William Hague, leader of the opposition, characterised the government's plans for removing the hereditary peers as 'constitutional vandalism', and argued that people would want to hear the conclusions of the royal commission before proceeding with stage one of reform. Hague thus exploited the soft underbelly of the two-stage process and laid the groundwork for Conservative opposition to the government's proposals when he asserted that: '[t]he reason the Prime Minister does not want to wait for the royal commission is clear: he has never intended carrying out proper reform of the House of Lords, but wants to create a house of cronies beholden to him alone'.[10] This two-pronged line of reasoning continued in the Commons' debate on the queen's speech, when Sir Norman Fowler argued that the government's intention was 'to introduce an assembly of appointees and placemen: a giant, ermine-clad quango', which would fail to put pressure on the government because such appointees would be 'very content with their lot', and contended that it was 'utterly absurd' to proceed with legislation in advance of either the government's white paper or the conclusion of the royal commission.[11]

The opposition was also able to make much of the fact that, in the summer of 1998, the government leader of the house of lords, Lord Richard, was fired because he was thought to be too strongly in favour of a substantially-elected second chamber, and was,

---

[8] Wheeler-Booth, 'The House of Lords', 654.

[9] Hansard, *Lords Debates*, 5th ser., dxcv, col. 4: 24 Nov. 1998.

[10] Hansard, *Commons Debates*, 6th ser., cccxxi, col. 24: 24 Nov. 1998.

[11] Hansard, *Commons Debates*, 6th ser., cccxxi, cols 560, 564, 565: 30 Nov. 1998.

thus, at odds with the prime minister and much of the cabinet.[12] Conservative MP, Kenneth Clarke, for example, was a known advocate of an elected element in the second chamber, but in arguing this case for the reformed Lords,[13] strategically illustrated the deep divisions within the government regarding the merits of having elected peers in the upper House. This, along with the absence of any coherent plan for what would happen in the putative stage two of reform, set the scene for the legislative process that accompanied the House of Lords Bill.

The House of Lords Bill was formally introduced into the house of commons on 19 January 1999, but the contentious nature of the legislation had already been revealed well before that date. Throughout 1998, secret talks took place between the Labour and Conservative leaders in the house of lords (Lord Richard and Lord Cranborne respectively), at the prompting of the prime minister, aimed at finding some kind of bipartisan approach to reform.[14] The central fear was that the Conservatives would abandon the Salisbury convention and oppose the legislation in the second chamber, thus causing a scenario in which the government was forced to use the Parliament Acts in order to remove the hereditary peers. It was exactly this kind of protracted constitutional battle which the government was keen to avoid. In addition, it was hoped that the secret negotiations would prepare the groundwork for a possible 'big bang' approach to reform whereby the government would delay removing all the hereditary peers in exchange for Conservative support for an at least partly-elected second chamber.[15] However, the complete absence of any united Labour government position with respect to the merits of an elected Lords, and the deep reservations of the prime minister himself on the matter, meant that the talks yielded little by way of an agreed approach on future composition.

None the less, the talks did succeed in mapping a way forward for the elimination of the hereditary peers. Working with Lord Irvine, following Lord Richard's sacking, Lord Cranborne promised to neutralise the threat of the Conservative peers destroying the government's reform agenda (by voting down the plans to remove the hereditary peers) in exchange for some of those peers being allowed to remain in the House. By November 1998, Cranborne had secured government agreement on retaining 92 hereditary peers. This comprised 75 (one-tenth of the hereditary peerage) who would be chosen by elections in which only the hereditary peers would be eligible to participate; 15 hereditary peers, who were to be available to serve as officeholders (such as deputy speaker) to ensure the efficient functioning of the House during the impending interim period, and who were to be elected by all peers; and two hereditary officers of state: the earl marshal and the lord great chamberlain.

However, Cranborne was caught unawares when his own shadow cabinet refused to support the plan he had worked out with Irvine.[16] Cranborne, not to be put off,

---

[12] Donald Shell, 'Labour and the House of Lords: A Case Study in Constitutional Reform', *Parliamentary Affairs*, liii (2000), 290–310.

[13] Hansard, *Commons Debates*, 6th ser., cccxxi, col. 580: 30 Nov. 1998.

[14] Michael Cockerell, 'The Politics of Second Chamber Reform: A Case Study of the House of Lords and the Passage of the House of Lords Act 1999', *Journal of Legislative Studies*, vii (2001), 119–34.

[15] Shell, 'Labour and the House of Lords', 298.

[16] Shell, 'Labour and the House of Lords', 300; Cockerell, 'The Politics of Second Chamber Reform', 124.

'smuggled himself into Number 10, to discuss the deal directly with Tony Blair'.[17] That meeting produced final agreement that the Conservative peers would not oppose the government so long as a number of hereditary members could remain in the house of lords. However, the leader of the Conservative Party, William Hague, was allegedly in the dark about Cranborne's secret meeting with Blair, and, upon finding out about it, attempted to blow the deal out of the water by exposing it during prime minister's questions on 2 December 1998. This was the first that most Labour MPs knew of the deal to retain some hereditary peers,[18] but the strategy of trying to instigate civil war in the Labour Party backfired, because Blair simply pointed out that if some hereditary peers remained, then it was because the Conservative leadership in the Lords has agreed to such a scenario. Blair undermined Hague's attempt to derail the deal by arguing that:

> even when hereditary Conservative peers are prepared to agree to change, the right hon. Gentleman is not. That is the absurd position to which he has reduced himself . . . We have the opportunity to reform the House of Lords properly, and to establish a programme that will remove hereditary peers, but will allow us to do that on the broadest possible basis of agreement. It is clear that nowadays, even when we speak to the leader of the Conservative party in the House of Lords, we cannot be sure that the leader of the Conservative party in this House is of the same mind.[19]

What then followed was tantamount to political farce. Although Hague fired Cranborne for agreeing to the deal with Tony Blair without his knowledge or approval, he appointed Lord Strathclyde as his successor, who had not only known about and supported Cranborne's deal, but was instructed by Hague to honour it. Consequently, before legislation had even been introduced into parliament, the entire process was already mired in controversy and the basic task of removing the hereditary peers had become hugely contentious.

None the less, by the time the legislative stages of the House of Lords Bill began, the new leader of the house of lords, Baroness Jay, had already secured the co-operation of the cross-bench peer, Lord Weatherill, to introduce the agreed amendment to reprieve the 92 hereditary peers agreed by Cranborne and Irvine. Weatherill had been working on his own amendment along similar lines, but was persuaded to substitute it for the Cranborne-Irvine plan instead, on the grounds that his seniority and standing in the Lords would help demonstrate the consensus position which the amendment sought to locate. With the amendment backed by the cross benches, the Conservative peers would be in a far easier position to abstain from the vote, and thus ensure that the legislation could be secured without undue constitutional fuss. Consequently, the government white paper published in December 1998, which outlined the removal of the hereditary peers and the creation of the royal commission on future reform, acknowledged that it would accept an amendment to reprieve the 92 peers if it meant that stage one of reform could be secured consensually.[20]

[17] Cockerell, 'The Politics of Second Chamber Reform', 124.

[18] Shell, 'Labour and the House of Lords', 300.

[19] Hansard, *Commons Debates*, 6th ser., cccxxi, col. 876: 3 Dec. 1998.

[20] Cabinet Office, *Modernising Parliament: Reforming the House of Lords*, Cm. 4183 (1999).

3. *The Legislative Process in the Commons*

The House of Lords Bill was purposefully short and simple, with the most important clause stating plainly that: 'No one shall be a member of the House of Lords by virtue of a hereditary peerage.' The second reading debate took place in the Commons on 1 and 2 February 1999. Although the leader of the Commons, Margaret Beckett, promoted the bill on the basis of its 'exquisite simplicity' in removing the hereditary peers,[21] and while many Labour MPs kept their contributions to the limited issue of the hereditary peers, much of the debate, nevertheless, focused on two problematic issues: first, the politics of the Weatherill amendment to reprieve some of the hereditary peers, and, second, the far more contentious issue of what would follow this stage one of reform.

The basic mechanics of the amendment to allow some hereditary peers to remain proved to be hugely controversial. Margaret Beckett acknowledged the agreement which had been reached to accept an amendment put forward by the cross benches in the Lords to reprieve 92 peers, and stated that the government was 'minded to accept it' so long as the rest of the government's legislative programme was not frustrated.[22] However, she also made it plain that the government would not accept a similarly-worded amendment if it was moved in the Commons instead.[23] Ostensibly, the reason for this was to ensure the good behaviour of the house of lords on the matter. However, the whole question of why the government was permitting the amendment, instead of incorporating it into the legislation at the start, beautifully illustrated the basis of the opposition that the Conservative Party was able to mount against the House of Lords Bill. Its own senior peers had played an integral role in bringing the reprieve amendment about. However, Conservatives in the house of commons were able to exploit the willingness of the government to allow the second chamber to constrain its constitutional legislation, without courting accusations of incoherence themselves, precisely because the Conservative leadership in the Commons had not been party to the negotiating process. The strange positioning of the Conservatives on the matter meant that it was, ironically, the government which found itself in the position of arguing that the hereditary peers were 'utterly, totally, literally, indefensible',[24] while simultaneously defending the arrangement to keep some of them in place for an interim period of unknown duration.

The second controversial issue which permeated the second reading debate concerned the process of reform following the removal of the hereditary peers. The Conservative MP, John Bercow, for example, asked Margaret Beckett if 'she expects reform to be completed within her remaining political lifetime', to which she replied in the affirmative,[25] a response which looked shaky at the time, and which looks even shakier a decade on, but which was, in fact, the only response that could have been offered. Despite Beckett's argument that consideration of stage two could only usefully proceed once the hereditary membership had been dealt with and the impact of the Conservative Party on

---

[21] Hansard, *Commons Debates*, 6th ser., cccxxiv, col. 609: 1 Feb. 1999.

[22] Hansard, *Commons Debates*, 6th ser., cccxxiv, col. 609: 1 Feb. 1999.

[23] Hansard, *Commons Debates*, 6th ser., cccxxiv, col. 610: 1 Feb. 1999.

[24] Hansard, *Commons Debates*, 6th ser., cccxxiv, col. 611: 1 Feb. 1999.

[25] Hansard, *Commons Debates*, 6th ser., cccxxiv, col. 612: 1 Feb. 1999.

the second chamber had been, at least somewhat, reined in,[26] the fact remained that this was an entirely new argument fashioned to justify the compromise that had been reached with the Conservative peers and which had never formed part of the Labour government's plans. In this respect, then, the government found itself in tricky political waters throughout the parliamentary process of enacting the House of Lords Bill, principally because the bill was a compromise which emphatically breached the Labour Party's manifesto commitment. The tone of the Commons' debate belied the deep concerns that existed not only across, but also within, the parties, most notably the Labour Party, whose members had, after all, been under the impression, as late as December 1998, that they were going to remove *all* hereditary peers from the second chamber. The realization that this was no longer official party policy, at least in the short term, consequently led many Labour MPs to question the veracity of the party's longer-term commitment to Lords' reform.

Fundamentally, although the government's political strategy was to separate stage one from stage two, its refusal to state its own preference for what a fully-reformed second chamber would ultimately look like, and then to defend that preference, gave much firepower to the opposition parties in the Commons. The government, of course, explained that it had not indicated a preference because it wanted to wait for the outcome of the royal commission inquiry, and that: 'it would be insulting to ask it to consider all those matters having stated what the end process should be'.[27] To the extent that the House of Lords Bill was a parliamentary done deal before it was even introduced, the only feasible opposition strategy was to abandon all serious defence of the hereditary principle (the Conservatives had, in fact, defended the hereditary principle in the house of lords in the 1997 election campaign), and focus instead on the evident divisions within the Labour Party with respect to the increasingly symbolic stage two. And what the second reading debate demonstrated was the variety of views which existed on the Labour benches about what a fully-reformed second chamber should look like in compositional terms. The different kinds of options outlined during the debate are too numerous and diverse to list here, covering a range of combinations of elected and appointed elements, with various arguments forwarded about how an elected membership would impact on the legitimacy of the House, all of which illustrated the difficulty the government could expect if it decided to pursue one single compositional option at some future point without ensuring its own back benchers were on board. The idea of creating a unicameral parliament was even broached seriously at this time,[28] an issue which was to have a significant impact on subsequent reform processes. Also under scrutiny was the extent to which the government would adhere to the recommendations of the royal commission once its report was published, and whether or not it was useful to have such a commission if the government planned to pursue a particular reform strategy regardless of what it said,[29] a point made by the former prime minister, John Major, on the second day of the debate. On this point, the veteran Labour MP, Tony Benn, argued that, given the 'immensely complex' deliberations of the royal commission

[26] Hansard, *Commons Debates*, 6th ser., cccxxiv, col. 616: 1 Feb. 1999.

[27] Hansard, *Commons Debates*, 6th ser., cccxxiv, col. 696: 1 Feb. 1999.

[28] Hansard, *Commons Debates*, 6th ser., cccxxiv, col. 644: 1 Feb. 1999.

[29] Hansard, *Commons Debates*, 6th ser., cccxxiv, col. 746: 2 Feb. 1999.

and any future joint committee, and the 'complex legislation' that would be required to enact compositional reform, there was a genuine fear that the interim House 'will become the permanent solution'.[30] None the less, the important division on the second reading saw a comfortable outcome for the government, and the bill passed by 381 votes to 135, and passed its third reading debate on 16 March 1999 by 340 votes to 132.

4. *The Legislative Process in the Lords*

Once the House of Lords Bill was safely in the second chamber, where it arrived on 17 March 1999, things became rather more complicated, and it was at this point in the legislative process that the content of the bill underwent the most change. In his opening remarks on the second reading debate, Lord Cranborne noted that the only certainty about the whole reform process was that 'no one expects this Bill in this form to become law',[31] and continued the Conservative attack on the legislation on the grounds that it pre-empted the royal commission and that the government had to be in a position to state what stage two would involve before embarking on stage one. Cranborne also softened up the ground for the Weatherill amendment, stating that retaining some hereditary peers would ensure that the government had to complete the reform process, while also placating the Conservative hereditary membership by arguing that the amendment 'falls well short of making the Bill acceptable'.[32] Lord Weatherill defended the amendment that bore his name on the grounds that it would facilitate stage one, on which the government had a clear manifesto commitment, and it would also 'provide some kind of reassurance of the Government's seriousness of intent to proceed to stage two'.[33]

However, the Weatherill amendment was not the only issue on which the house of lords had to reflect. Michael Cockerell, then a BBC journalist observing the removal of the hereditary peers for a documentary series, outlined the work undertaken by the bill team as it attempted to deal with the various amendments put forward by hereditary peers 'who were masters of parliamentary procedure'.[34] Lord Falconer told Cockerell that 'the way the opposition went in the Bill, unlike any other Bill I'd ever seen, was it became an incredibly sort of intense legal debate, with frankly mad legal propositions being advanced'. One of those related to an amendment from Earl Ferrers, about whether the word 'hereditary' should be preceded by 'a' or 'an', with the bill team and the house of lords having no choice but to commit time to the discussion of such amendments to ensure that the legislation could stand up to legal scrutiny.

Of potentially more importance, though, were two particular issues about the broader implications of the bill with respect to its likely effects, issues which delayed its continued progress. The first related to the language used to refer to hereditary peers in the bill, and the legalities of the writ of summons. Lord Mayhew of Twysden argued that the language

[30] Hansard, *Commons Debates*, 6th ser., cccxxiv, col. 746: 2 Feb. 1999.

[31] Hansard, *Lords Debates*, 5th ser., dxcix, col. 17: 29 Mar. 1999.

[32] Hansard, *Lords Debates*, 5th ser., dxcix, col. 20: 29 Mar. 1999.

[33] Hansard, *Lords Debates*, 5th ser., dxcix, col. 215: 30 Mar. 1999.

[34] Cockerell, 'The Politics of Second Chamber Reform', 127–8.

was 'uncertain in its effects and would leave the position of most hereditary Peers uncertain if the Bill was enacted'.[35] The second issue related to whether the House of Lords Bill, once enacted, would breach the provisions of the treaty of union of 1707. Lord Gray argued that a fundamental element of the union between England and Scotland was that the latter had hereditary representation in the house of lords guaranteed by statute, and that if there was no such representation, then the treaty of union would be breached.[36] The house of lords referred both these matters to the committee for privileges. Although this committee decided that there was no case to answer with either of these concerns,[37] it did not report until after the summer recess, and it was, therefore, October 1999 before these legal matters had been resolved to the satisfaction of the upper House.

None the less, the effective substance of the House of Lords Bill was altered, not only by the government's acceptance of the Weatherill amendment which reprieved 92 hereditary peers, but also because of the nuance of that amendment and its longer-term implications. The government, not wishing its short, simple bill to be complicated by electoral arrangements for the reprieved peers, passed the question off to the house of lords' procedure committee, which reported in July 1999, and outlined new House standing orders to facilitate the Weatherill amendment provisions.[38] These new standing orders essentially outlined a series of complex electoral arrangements through which the 15 places for officeholders would be elected by all peers, while the remaining 75 places would be divided up between the parties, and the reprieved peers from each party would be chosen separately by the hereditary peers from those parties. However, the Weatherill amendment also ensured that when a reprieved hereditary peer died, he or she would be replaced by means of a by-election, with the eligible candidates comprising excluded peers. This mechanism was pursued in order to ensure that the total number of hereditary peers inside the second chamber remained fixed at 92 until the second stage of reform could be secured, and so that the inclusion of the reprieved hereditary peers was not undone over time as they die.

Donald Shell observed of these electoral mechanisms for the hereditary peers that 'a major measure of constitutional reform has been enacted making provision of such nonsense' and that 'the report of the Lords Procedure Committee that drew up these rules must be considered one of the most hilarious documents ever published by such a body'.[39] Indeed, when reading the procedure committee minutes and discussions on this matter, and the various analyses of whether life peers should be permitted to participate in the elections, it is difficult not to think that the whole thing was some kind of constitutional joke. Yet, so keen was the government to get the House of Lords Bill onto the statute book, and so much did it apparently fear that the hereditary peers might well snap around at the last possible moment and vote the whole thing down, that it was seemingly willing to agree to all kinds of parliamentary foolishness that must surely have

[35] Hansard, *Lords Debates*, 5th ser., dciv, col. 1397: 27 July 1999.

[36] Hansard, *Lords Debates*, 5th ser., dciv, col. 1420: 27 July 1999.

[37] House of Lords Select Committee for Privileges, First Report of Session 1998–99, HL Paper 106 (1999); Second Report of Session 1998–99, HL Paper 108 (1999).

[38] House of Lords Select Committee on Procedure of the House, Third Report of Session 1998–99, HL Paper 81 (1999).

[39] Shell, 'Labour and the House of Lords', 305.

had the more seasoned of the hereditary peers doubled over with mirth. None the less, these provisions within the Weatherill amendment ensured that the house of lords approved the bill at third reading by 221 votes to 81, with the vast bulk of the Conservative peers abstaining from the vote.

5. *Constitutional and Parliamentary Consequences*

One of the most bizarre, and certainly unintended, constitutional consequences of the House of Lords Act, which reached the statute books on 11 November 1999, was that it brought a hugely questionable form of democracy into the second chamber, whereby hereditary peers, although excluded by law from sitting and voting in the Lords, could still gain membership of it under that same act if their hereditary colleagues voted for them either in the elections which took place in 1999 or in a by-election upon the death of one of the reprieved peers. That this arrangement could be put in place, given that the original intentions of the Labour Party were to remove all of the hereditary peers completely, demonstrates the irrational fear which gripped the Labour government after just a year in office. Despite its towering Commons' majority, and the obvious use it could make of the rhetoric surrounding its mandate to implement a manifesto commitment, the Labour government, nevertheless, shrank from proceeding unilaterally even with the limited task of removing the hereditary peers, a task against which it was almost impossible to argue from the perspective of modern representative democracy. So eager was it to find consensus, and thus avoid a constitutional impasse which could be resolved only by using the Parliament Acts, that it did not really stop to consider whether there was anything behind the threat from the hereditary peers to hold up the government's legislative programme if it tried to evict them from the second chamber. Given the popularity of the Labour government at that time, it is doubtful whether such a strategy, if utilised, would have resulted in anything other than a huge public backlash against the hereditary peers and an unequivocal government victory with added political capital to boot.

Yet, even after the House of Lords Act was passed, there remained the far more complicated question of what stage two of reform would look like and when it would happen. In the decade after the hereditary peers were expelled from the second chamber, there was no further compositional reform in the house of lords, despite several attempts to secure it. In casting Lords' reform in terms of a two-stage approach, it became inevitable that a major consequence of (partially) securing stage one would be constant questioning about stage two. The report of the royal commission on the reform of the house of lords was published in January 2000, and recommended a largely-appointed chamber.[40] The report was not well-received in the media,[41] nor was the government's subsequent commitment to a policy in which elected members would be in a minority in a reformed Lords.[42] In 2002, the reformist leader of the house of commons, Robin

[40] Royal Commission on the Reform of the House of Lords, *A House for the Future*, Cm. 4534 (2000).
[41] Alexandra Kelso, *Parliamentary Reform at Westminster* (Manchester, 2009), 162.
[42] Cabinet Office, *The House of Lords: Completing the Reform*, Cm. 5291 (2001).

Cook, attempted to upend the government's policy on a nominated chamber[43] by appointing a joint committee on reform of the house of lords, some six years after it had been promised in the 1997 election manifesto. A house of commons' public adminis-tration committee report published in February 2002 had located a 'centre of gravity' amongst MPs for a second chamber that was at least 60% elected.[44] The joint committee was given the task of acting on this finding by formulating a series of options for different kinds of composition, and outlining the various advantages and disadvantages of each, in preparation for parliamentary votes on them which, Cook hoped, would result in a clearly-expressed preference of what most MPs would consider to be an acceptable composition in the upper House. The joint committee's report,[45] which outlined seven options ranging from fully appointed to fully elected, and with different mixed propor-tions in between (for example, 60% elected, 40% nominated, and *vice versa*) was debated in parliament on 4 February 2003. However, the Commons was unable to unite behind any single compositional option in the division, with none of those on offer securing a majority, although the 80% elected option was defeated by just three votes.[46] The entire process consequently ended in total farce, and demonstrated not only the anxiety that gripped the Commons about what an elected second chamber might mean for its own democratic legitimacy, but also the extent to which raw politics dictated the outcome of the 2003 vote, with the Conservative Party working specifically in order to embarrass the government over the entire Lords' reform affair, and with a significant minority of MPs promoting a unicameral option, the strength of support for which surprised the front benches.[47] Further such embarrassment was secured in March 2007, near the end of the Westminster career of prime minister Tony Blair, when another Commons' vote this time backed a 100% and an 80% elected second chamber with majorities of 113 and 38 respectively, although the strategic voting behaviour of MPs in favour of a unicameral parliament also inflated these numbers in order to complicate things for the govern-ment.[48] This support for an elected House was not only a massive reversal of the 2003 outcome, but was also a substantial snub to Blair, whose own preferences for a largely-nominated second chamber had stalled progress on stage two throughout his premier-ship. It also corresponded with the imminent arrival of the new prime minister, Gordon Brown, whose own preferences for an elected chamber were well known. Despite this, it was not until near the end of his premiership that the house of lords was addressed, in the Constitutional Reform and Governance Bill 2008–9. Yet, this did not seek to take forward stage two, nor even speedily to complete stage one, but, instead, aimed to secure the far more limited task of ending the process of hereditary peer by-elections, thus facilitating their eventual removal through atrophy. In the event, even these provisions were lost in the parliamentary 'wash-up' at the end of the session.

[43] Robin Cook, *The Point of Departure* (2003), 78.

[44] Public Administration Select Committee, *The Second Chamber: Continuing the Reform*, Fifth Report of Session 2001–02, HC 494–1 (2002).

[45] Joint Committee on House of Lords Reform, *House of Lords Reform*, First Report of Session 2001–02, HL Paper 17, HC 171 (2002).

[46] I. McLean, A. Spirling and M. Russell, 'None of the Above: The UK House of Commons Votes on Reforming the House of Lords, February 2003', *Political Quarterly*, lxxiv (2003), 298–310.

[47] Kelso, *Parliamentary Reform at Westminster*, 175.

[48] Kelso, *Parliamentary Reform at Westminster*, 179.

Consequently, although the incoming Labour government in 1997 pledged to remove all the hereditary peers and then consider more fundamental compositional reform, the fact remains that, at the end of their time in office, a major point of contention concerned the continued existence of some hereditary peers in parliament and the total lack of political will on the part of the government to continue the process of reform. Indeed, had the government been as bold with house of lords' reform as it had been with devolution, the complexion of Westminster would be quite different today, and the basis on which second chamber reform discussions take place would be rather different also.

There is yet another consequence of the House of Lords Act 1999 which has slightly different implications. To the extent that there was no clearly worked-out plan for stage two, opponents of stage one were able to argue during the parliamentary debates that accompanied the House of Lords Act that stripping the hereditary peers from the second chamber left it 'much more in the power of the serving Prime Minister, and would make it a party political machine supporting the Government in power'.[49] The idea that stage one would simply create a House of 'Tony's cronies' which the Labour government would be happy to maintain, because the interim House was a pushover as far as legislation was concerned, was a compelling argument when it was made in 1999, but one which has not turned out to be accurate. Research has demonstrated that, far from becoming a more subservient chamber, the house of lords has become far more assertive since the removal of most of the hereditary peers, has an increasingly important impact on government policy, and offers far more scrutiny obstacles to legislation than does the house of commons.[50] While the issue of how legitimacy is conceived is a difficult one,[51] the life peers, nevertheless, seem to feel less encumbered with the hereditary peers removed, and more willing to fulfil the broad range of parliamentary functions ascribed to the second chamber.

This has impacted on the continued debate about what a reformed second chamber should look like in compositional terms. With the house of lords increasingly demonstrating the valuable task it performs in the legislative process, those opposed to an elected chamber are now in possession of mounting evidence about the capability and utility of an appointed chamber at Westminster, evidence which those who favour an elected House must formulate increasingly convincing arguments against. Therefore, a major consequence of the House of Lords Act 1999, and the two-stage process of reform in which it was embedded, is that it brought about an interim House which was hugely capable of demonstrating its functional value. None the less, despite the failure to proceed to stage two, removal of most of the hereditary peers from the second chamber in itself represented a massive constitutional change for Westminster, and proved that parliamentary reform need not always be incremental.

[49] Hansard, *Commons Debates*, 6th ser, cccxxiv, col. 643: 1 Feb. 1999.

[50] M. Russell and M. Sciara, 'The Policy Impact of Defeats in the House of Lords', *British Journal of Politics and International Relations*, x (2008), 571–89.

[51] A. Kelso, 'Reforming the House of Lords: Navigating Representation, Democracy and Legitimacy at Westminster', *Parliamentary Affairs*, lix (2006), 563–81.

Index